GOOD VIBES, GOOD LIFE

GOOD

HOW SELF-LOVE IS

VIBES,

THE KEY TO UNLOCKING

GOOD

YOUR GREATNESS

LIFE

VEX KING

HAY HOUSE

HAY HOUSE INDIA

New Delhi • London • Sydney
Carlsbad, California • New York City

Hay House Publishers (India) Pvt Ltd
Muskaan Complex, Plot No. 3, B-2, Vasant Kunj, New Delhi – 110070, India

Hay House LLC, P.O. Box 5100, Carlsbad, CA 92018-5100, USA
Hay House UK Ltd, 1st Floor, Crawford Corner, 91-93 Baker Street, London W1U 6QQ, UK
Hay House Australia Publishing Pty Ltd, 18/36 Ralph St., Alexandria NSW 2015, Australia

Email: contact@hayhouse.co.in
Website: www.hayhouse.co.in

ISBN 978-93-86832-83-2

First published by Hay House India, 2019
Reprint, 2025
36 35 34 33 32 31 30 29 28 27

Printed at Thomson Press

FSC www.fsc.org MIX Paper | Supporting responsible forestry FSC® C010615

Hay House is committed to a sustainable future for our business, our readers and our planet. This book is made from Forest Stewardship Council® certified paper.

Mum, I dedicate this book to you. Our life has been tough, but with your strength, faith and perseverance, you've made incredible things happen for us.

Regardless of everything that came your way and all the times I've let you down, you've shown me nothing but unconditional love. It was this love that led to the sacrifices that you made, and it was this love that kept me smiling. You forgave, you hugged, you laughed, you inspired, you encouraged, you healed, and you did everything else in your power to demonstrate that with love, anything was possible. Which is why I'm here today, passing on my love to others, through my words.

And Dad – of course, my existence would not be possible without you. Although I never got to know you properly, I've always felt your energy guiding me when I needed it most. I know how much I meant to you when I was born. I hope you're proud of me.

Finally, I'd like to dedicate this book to anyone with a dream, whether that's a dream just to survive, or to make it through a dark day. It was my dream to write a book that will positively change lives across the world. If I can make it happen, so can you. I believe in you – I hope you do, too.

Contents

Introduction

For three years of my childhood, I had no fixed home. My family and I lived with relatives and, for short periods during this time, in a housing shelter. I was grateful that we had a roof over our heads, but I remember how frightening the housing shelter experience was.

There were always unpleasant-looking characters lurking around the entrance who would throw us piercing stares when we entered the building. Being a four-year-old child, I felt scared. But my mother reassured me that things would be okay. She said that we should just look down and go straight to our room.

One night we popped out, and when we returned there was blood all over the staircase and on the walls in the corridor. Fragments of glass covered the floor. My sisters and I had never seen anything so horrific before. We looked up at our mum. I sensed fear in her. But again, with courage, she told us to tread carefully over the glass and get up to our room.

Still shaken by what we'd seen, my sisters and I tried to work out what may have happened downstairs in the corridor of the shelter. Then we heard screams and shouting, followed by sounds of chaos. It was terrifying. Once more, we looked to Mum for comfort. She pulled us in close and told us not to worry – but I could hear her heart pounding. She was just as scared.

We had very little sleep that night. The screams went on and on. I was surprised that no police came and that no one else seemed to be trying to calm the storm. It was as though no one cared about the safety of the people there. It felt like no one cared about us. All we had was each other, in a world that seemed cold and corrupt.

When I discuss childhood memories like this one with my friends and family, they're shocked by how much I can remember. I often find them asking, 'How do you even remember that? You were so young.' I don't remember everything, nor are my memories crystallized in clear detail. However, I do remember how I felt during the majority of my experiences, good and bad. There was so much emotion attached to the events that took place, and these memories haunted me for a very long time.

During my late teens, I wished a lot of these memories would just go away. I wanted to erase them so that I was no longer reminded of the struggles I'd faced as a child. I was even embarrassed by some of them. I felt uncomfortable with who I was. There were times when I said and did things that didn't match the child I was deep down. I often felt hurt by the world – and wanted to hurt it back.

Things are different now. I look back on my memories and embrace everything that happened; there's a lesson to be learned from every event.

I realize that the good, the bad and the downright ugly events are all a part of who I've become.

Although some of them may have been painful, they're a blessing – they've taught me so much. My experiences have left me with a drive to find a way out of misery and a path towards a better life.

I've written this book to share the lessons I've learned, in the hope that they'll provide you with some clarity and guidance to live what I call *a greater life*. It's up to you what you take from my stories. I accept that some ideas will resonate, while others will feel uncomfortable. Nevertheless, I do believe that if you can apply the concepts I discuss within the course of this book, you'll experience incredible positive changes in your life.

I'm not a philosopher, a psychologist, a scientist or a religious leader. I'm simply someone who likes to learn and share my wisdom with others in the hope that it may release them from undesirable feelings and increase feelings of joy.

I believe that every person on this planet is here to make a difference. I'm devoted to helping you find your purpose so you can add value to our world, which is in such turmoil. If we can collectively become conscious citizens of this planet, we'll lessen the burden we place on it. By living to your full potential, you'll not only change your world, you'll change the world around you, too.

Some people are comfortable with mediocrity. They avoid living a greater life, one that's beyond what most consider the norm. A greater life requires you to find your greatness. In simple terms, greatness is about becoming the greatest version of yourself. It's about breaking the imaginary boundaries that hold you captive in a life you believe you have to settle for, and touching the realms of the unthinkable. The greatness mentality means living a life without limits, where there are infinite possibilities. For this reason, we cannot define where greatness begins or ends. We can only strive to become better.

Stop trying to impress people.
Impress yourself.
Stretch yourself.
Test yourself.
Be the best version of you that you can be.

This book requires you to commit to a better you *right now*. My aim is to help you become better than the person you were yesterday, every day, in each and every way, for the rest of your life. If you wake up with this desire in your mind and then consciously follow up on it, you'll be surprised by how much inspiration you find. Your life will begin to reflect your commitment to progress.

Greatness isn't a one-dimensional term. Although it's subjective, most will associate the word with having a special talent, lots of money or material possessions, authority or status, and big achievements under their belt. But true greatness goes deeper than that. It cannot exist without purpose, love, selflessness, humility, appreciation, kindness and, of course – our highest priority as human beings – happiness. When I think of greatness, I think of reaching a level of mastery across all avenues of life and making a positive impact on the world. Great people aren't just the high rollers in life, but those who we value as amazing inhabitants of this world.

You deserve a greater life and this book will help you create it.

DAILY GOAL

'Be better than who I was yesterday.'

Post pictures or your favourite images, pages, quotes and experiences related to this book on social media using #**VexKingBook** so I can like them and feature them on my page.

What is self-love?

To achieve a sense of peace, we need balance: balance between work and play, between action and patience, spending and saving, laughter and seriousness, leaving and staying. Failing to achieve a balance across every area of your life can leave you feeling exhausted, among many other unpleasant emotions, such as guilt.

Here's an example of balancing action and patience. If you're the project leader of a final-year university assignment and you catch a team member who you like on social media instead of helping your team, you may allow it to slide. If they do it on multiple occasions and you notice their productivity slipping, you may warn them that if it persists, you'll have to report them to your course leader. If they then choose to ignore you and continue their behaviour, would you feel guilty about taking further action?

If you're a kind and compassionate human being, you may fear hurting their feelings and getting them in trouble. By reporting them to the course leader, they may have to face severe consequences that affect their final grade and that might have implications on their future. However, they're disrespecting you and ignoring your warnings. You may feel like they're taking your kindness for granted. And you might worry that other project members will be disheartened if they see your lenience as favouritism.

In this instance, if you're kind and honest, and follow a fair process, you needn't feel guilty for taking further action.

It's important to recognize that it's not unjust to let go of those who show no concern for you.

As project leader, you can remember that you tried your best, and unfortunately, your friend chose not to respond. If you don't take action, you risk losing your inner peace, the respect of your team and harming your own final grade.

By taking a balanced approach, you can feel more at ease and avoid any bad feelings, such as guilt. You demonstrate both action and patience. You can show that you're understanding and forgiving,

Self-love is the balance between
accepting yourself as you are
while knowing you deserve better,
and then working towards it.

and also firm and authoritative. The chances are that even if this student is upset by your decision, they will still respect you for giving them a chance.

So, what does this have to do with self-love? Well, the phrase 'self-love' is often misunderstood. Self-love encourages acceptance, but many people use this as an excuse to remain unchallenged. In fact, self-love consists of two essential elements that must be balanced if one wishes to live a harmonious life.

The first element encourages unconditional love towards yourself. The focus is on mindset. The truth is, you won't love yourself more if, for example, you lose or gain weight, or undergo cosmetic surgery. You may feel more confident, sure. But true self-love is when you appreciate where you are and who you are, regardless of any transformation you aspire to.

The second element encourages growth, and the focus is on taking action. Improving yourself and your life is also self-love because it means you recognize that you deserve more than settling for mediocrity.

When it comes to self-love, think about what it means to love others unconditionally. For example, your partner may have annoying habits, but this doesn't mean you love them any less.

You accept them as they are, and sometimes even learn from their flaws. You also want what's best for them. Therefore, if a particular habit was affecting their health, you'd support them in making positive changes. This demonstrates your unconditional love for them. You don't judge them harshly, but you do want them to be the best version of themselves – for their own sake. Self-love is about applying this to yourself: having your own best interests at heart.

True self-love can be present in anything that adds value to your life, from your diet to your spiritual rituals or the way you interact within your personal relationships. And, of course, a significant aspect of self-love is acceptance: being content with who you are, as you are. As a result, self-love is empowerment and liberation.

An understanding of self-love allows us to find balance between mindset and action. Without balance we'll regularly stumble, fall and feel lost. When you love yourself, life will begin to love you back.

The balance between mindset and action will enable you to vibrate higher. We'll explore this further in the next few chapters.

You accept them as they are, and sometimes even learn from their ways. You also want what's best for them. Therefore, if a particular habit was affecting their health, you'd support them to make positive changes. This doesn't alter your unconditional love for them. You don't judge them harshly, but you do want them to be the best version of themselves — for their own sake. Self-love is about applying this to yourself, having your own best interests at heart.

True self-love can be present in anything that adds value to your life, be it your diet, your spiritual beliefs or the way you interact within your personal relationships. And, of course, a significant aspect of self-love is acceptance, being content with who you are as you are. As a result, self-love is empowerment and liberation.

An understanding of self-love allows us to find balance between mindset and action. Without balance we'll regularly stumble, fall and feel lost. When you love yourself, life will begin to love you back.

The balance between mindset and action will enable you to vibrate higher. We'll explore this further in the next few chapters.

PART ONE

A Matter of Vibes

Introduction

My time at university was a financial struggle. Although I'd been given a student loan, most of it went on my accommodation. I had very little to live on. I couldn't buy any course books because I couldn't afford them. I wouldn't ask my mum for money, because I knew she was struggling herself. I knew that if I did ask her, she'd somehow find the money for me as she had done her whole life, even if it meant that she couldn't eat.

For the most part I budgeted well. I could go out and party with my friends regularly, I never went hungry, and I didn't have to keep wearing the same clothes. I made a little money from online endeavours, like building customized page layouts on MySpace.

During one summer term I returned home for a break. I had no money left and everything felt hard. I didn't want to go back to university because I didn't enjoy the work and I had no motivation to complete my summer assignments. Having spent much of the year studying, I was forced to find a summer job so I'd be able stay afloat when I got back to university. All of my friends were planning a much-needed holiday together, and I couldn't afford to go. And I was having problems with a girl. The drama I was experiencing in my romantic and platonic relationships constantly angered me, and I didn't feel good about life.

One evening, I came across a book called *The Secret*.[1] People were saying it was changing their lives, and that *everyone* could benefit from it. It was founded on a simple principle: the Law of Attraction.

The premise of the Law of Attraction is that what you think about, you bring about. In other words, we can attract the things we want in our lives by committing our thoughts to them. This applies to the things you *don't* want, as well as to the things you *do* want; quite simply, whatever you focus on will be returned to you. So, the Law of Attraction stresses the importance of thinking about what you want, rather than focusing on things you fear or dread.

The Law of Attraction places great emphasis on positive thinking.

1 Byrne, R., *The Secret* (Simon and Schuster, 2006)

To me, it sounded too good to be true, so I began to do more research and I read about people who were claiming that the Law of Attraction was bringing them astonishing changes. Could I apply this to my life, too?

I knew exactly what I wanted: to go on holiday with my friends. I needed roughly £500 for this to happen. So I followed the general guidelines and tried to be as positive as I could.

A week or so later, I received a letter from the tax office saying that I may have paid too much tax. Was this a sign that the Law of Attraction was working? I filled out the form to provide them with further details and posted it back to them as soon as I could. A week went by and I heard nothing. My friends were getting ready to book their holiday, and I felt miserable that I wouldn't be able to join them. The potential of a tax rebate lingered in the back of my mind.

With growing frustration, I rang the tax office and asked them if they'd received my letter. They confirmed that they had, and that I'd hear back soon. At this point, I felt excited – but I was running out of time. The summer term was ending and my friends would be going away soon.

Another week went by and I still hadn't received anything. I was starting to give up on the idea and told my friends to book the holiday without me. I decided to focus elsewhere and lift my mood by reading motivational material. At least this would make me feel a little bit better about life.

A few more days passed, then an envelope from the tax office arrived. I opened it nervously. Inside was a cheque for £800. I was shocked, overwhelmed and overjoyed. I got myself to the bank as fast as I could to deposit the cheque. Cheques usually take up to five days to clear, but this one was in my account within three days.

The following Monday my friends and I booked a last-minute holiday and flew out four days later. I had a wonderful time. But, more importantly, I became a believer in the Law of Attraction.

I decided that I was going to use this to change my entire life.

There's something missing from the Law of Attraction

For the Law of Attraction to work, you have to think positively. However, it's difficult to stay positive all the time. When things go wrong in life, or they don't quite turn out how we expect, it's hard to remain optimistic.

Most people saw me as a positive individual. But when things got hard, I was far from it. Anger had always got the better of me. Sometimes, external events would create so much rage within me that I'd want to wreck everything in sight. As a result, I'd enter a downward spiral. I fluctuated constantly from highs to extreme lows. I was like two different people. These inconsistencies were projected onto my life. I'd go through some really good periods and then experience really bad ones. During the bad times, it was impossible to see the bright side of things. I tended to give in and take out my frustrations on the world by smashing up furniture, speaking rudely to others and moaning about how terrible it was to live in the world.

During my last year of university, I experienced a massive setback in a group project that counted for a significant percentage of my final grade, when my group became divided over how much of a contribution people were making. I tried to be optimistic about it and expected it to work out in the end. But it didn't – it got really messy.

It suddenly seemed clear that the Law of Attraction didn't always work. My group was completely divided, arguing constantly over our individual roles and how much effort each member was putting in, just months before graduation. Things got out of control and harsh words were exchanged; unfortunately, there was no way to fix the issue. My friend Darryl and I felt that we were treated very unfairly, but there wasn't much we could do about it, other than work ten times harder, with looming deadlines that seemed impossible to meet, especially on top of the rest of our workload. We were convinced we'd fail our assignments and exams, and therefore be unable to graduate. It felt like we'd wasted our entire time at university.

I had gone to university because I felt like I had to. It was what you were supposed to do if you wanted a good job and a comfortable life – which I hadn't experienced during my childhood. But deep down I didn't really want to be there. I didn't enjoy it. I always knew I wouldn't end up in a traditional job. I was doing this for my mum more than anything. I'd watched her struggle my whole life and wanted to show her it hadn't been in vain.

Now that I was so close to the finish line, it was all going to be taken away from me. All I could think about was letting my mum down, letting myself down and all the money wasted on a degree that I was going to fail. It was all for nothing. I was overcome by negative thoughts.

I told my mum I was going to leave university, as I had no reason to be there. I hated it and it was unfair what I was going through. My rage needed a scapegoat, so I blamed her for everything. Lovingly, she tried to convince me to stay and do the best I could, but in anger I only argued with her even more.

I was fed up with the endless problems and I wanted to leave everything behind. I had no reason to live and no purpose in life. My low state even led me to revisit some of my worst memories, which just added more fuel to the fire, convincing me that my life was worthless. What was the point in having dreams if I could never manifest them? I convinced myself I was living a lie and kidding myself that I could do big things.

It seemed clear right then: great things were never meant for me. So I trawled through employment websites and applied for a variety of jobs that looked fairly interesting and paid well, even though I wasn't qualified for them. I thought that if I could land one, I wouldn't seem like a complete failure and would at least have some money to help out my family with their debt, bills and expenses, including my sisters' weddings. In my covering letters, I explained that although I was underqualified, I'd be the perfect employee. No one responded.

Underneath it all, I knew I couldn't quit university when I'd already come so far. I'd expended so much energy trying to find a way out of the problem, but now it was time to face what had to be done and hope for the best.

But first I had my eldest sister's wedding to attend. This added more pressure. It meant that I'd have to hand in an assignment earlier than everyone else and take time off university just two months before my final deadlines, which would set me back even more. Stubbornly, I told my family that I couldn't go to the wedding, even though I knew I'd forever regret missing such an important event. In the end I did go – albeit reluctantly.

And soon as I got there, something unexpected happened. I felt calm and relaxed. The wedding was in Goa, India, and it was beautiful. Everyone there was shining bright with happiness and love for my sister and her new husband. Honestly, at this point I wasn't trying to feel positive. I was comfortable feeling down and feeling sorry for myself, and I wanted others to feel sorry for me, too. But this new environment created a welcome shift in me. For the first time in ages, I felt grateful.

I'll always remember my sister's wedding. And it taught me a lot about how the Universe operates.

On my return home, the positive feeling stayed with me. I felt good, and very calm about the chaos outside me. And my renewed steadiness motivated me to finish what needed to be done.

I created a dummy scorecard that displayed the overall mark I would receive for my degree. I'd stare at this for a few minutes each day while pretending that the impressive grade on the scorecard was real. I didn't quite believe that I'd achieve it; it was merely a desire. But I *did* believe that I would do well, nonetheless.

I made up my mind to go to the library every single day, for hours on end. I put in the huge amount of extra work needed to complete the group assignment, and more. During my breaks I took time to chat with positive people who were able to make me feel good about myself.

One of them was the woman I'd eventually fall in love with for life.

When it came to exam time, handing in assignments and doing final year presentations, I was confident that I'd done enough. As it turned out, I didn't quite get the marks that were on my dummy scorecard, but I did pass comfortably. And I aced one of the hardest exams on my course, which came as a surprise.

I went on to have similar successes by using the Law of Attraction. But, overall, the results were hit and miss. I knew I was missing something. When I found out what this was, I began to have more consistent success. I was able to test this on others, to see if they'd also benefit from my discovery – and they did. In fact, many of them were able to do things that had once seemed impossible.

Not everything I've wanted has manifested. This has usually been a blessing in disguise. Too many times I've believed that I wanted and needed something, but it was for all the wrong reasons. Over the years I've gained clarity and sighed with relief for not getting what I thought was surely meant for me. Often, I've not got what I wanted, only to find I've later been blessed with even more.

The Law of Vibration

The Universe responds to your vibration.
It will return whatever energy you put out.

Beyond the Law of Attraction is the Law of Vibration. It's the key component to a greater life. Once you learn and apply the ideas around this law, your life will transform. This isn't to say that you'll avoid all difficulties. What you will do, though, is find a way to take control and create a life that feels just as good as it looks.

One of the earliest authors of self-improvement literature is Napoleon Hill. His 1937 book, *Think and Grow Rich*,[2] remains one of the bestselling books of all time, and many of the world's entrepreneurial gurus praise its guidance to achieving success. Hill's research for his book included interviews with 500 successful men and women to find out what they'd done to attain their success –

2 Hill, N., *Think and Grow Rich: The Original 1937 Unedited Edition* (Napoleon Hill Foundation, 2012)

he then shared the wisdom he'd accumulated from them. Among his conclusions, he claimed: 'We are what we are, because of the vibrations of thought which we pick up and register, through the stimuli of our daily environment.' Hill makes many references to the concept of 'vibration' in his book, and you'll see the word 'vibration' (today commonly abbreviated to 'vibe') a number of times in my book, too.

Yet many later editions of Hill's book removed any mention of the word 'vibration'. Perhaps the publishers didn't believe the world was ready for Hill's concept. Even today, metaphysical laws related to vibration are under criticism due to a lack of scientific evidence. Despite this, there have been a number of attempts to explain the Law of Vibration. Scientists Dr Bruce Lipton and author Gregg Braden are among those at the forefront of bridging the gap between science and spirituality.[3] Their ideas on how our thoughts affect our lives support the concept suggested by the Law of Vibration, even if some believe it to be no more than modern pseudoscience.

Regardless, I for one have found that the Law of Vibration resonates deeply with me, and helps me make sense of life – and I know many

3 Lipton, B.H., *The Biology of Belief: Unleashing the Power of Consciousness, Matter and Miracles* (Hay House, 2015); brucelipton.com; greggbraden.com; 'Sacred knowledge of vibrations and water' (Gregg Braden on Periyad VidWorks, YouTube, August 2012)

others have discovered this, too. I've seen miraculous changes occur from using the Law of Vibration, and whether you become a believer or remain on the other side of the fence, throughout this book you'll learn that the Law of Vibration does no harm. Sometimes, first-hand experience is more valuable than any data measurable in numbers and graphs.

So what *is* the Law of Vibration?

To begin with, remember that everything is made up of atoms, and every atom is a little vibration. Therefore all matter and energy is vibrational by nature.

If you think back to school, you were taught that solids, liquids and gases are all different states of matter. The frequency of the vibrations at a molecular level defines what state they're in and how they appear to us.

Reality as we perceive it occurs through matching vibrations. In other words, for reality to be perceived, we have to be vibrationally compatible with it. The human ear, for example, will only hear sound waves that are between 20 and 20,000 vibrations per second. This doesn't mean that other sound waves don't exist; we just can't perceive them. When a dog whistle is blown, the frequency is above the vibrational range of the human ear and therefore doesn't exist to us.

In his book *The Vibrational Universe*,[4] spiritual author Kenneth James Michael MacLean writes that our five senses, our thoughts, as well as matter and energy, are *all* vibrational. He argues that reality is perception defined by vibrational interpretation. Our Universe is clearly a deep sea of vibrational frequencies, meaning that reality is a vibrational ether that's responsive to changes in vibration.

If the Universe is responsive to our thoughts, words, feelings and actions – because, according to MacLean, they're all vibrational – then it's assumed by the Law of Vibration that we can control our reality.

Change the way you think, feel, speak and act, and you begin to change your world.

To bring an idea into existence, or rather, into your perception, you must match its vibrational frequency. The more 'real' or solid something is to you, the closer you are to it vibrationally. This is why when you truly believe in something and act as if it were

4 MacLean, K.J.M., *The Vibrational Universe* (The Big Picture, 2005)

already true, you increase the chances of it coming to you in your physical reality.

To receive or perceive the reality you wish to have, you must be in energetic harmony with that which you desire. This means that our thoughts, emotions, words and actions must align with what we want.

This can be represented by taking two tuning forks that are calibrated to the same frequency. If you strike one of them so that it starts vibrating, the second fork will also vibrate while remaining untouched. The vibration from the struck tuning fork transfers to the untouched tuning fork because they're attuned to the same frequency: they're in vibrational harmony. If they're *not* in vibrational harmony, then the vibration of the struck tuning fork will not translate to the other.

Similarly, to listen to a specific radio station you have to tune the receiver to the frequency of that station. This is the only way you can hear it. If you tune in to a different frequency, you'll end up listening to a completely different station.

Once you're in vibrational resonance with something, you begin to attract it into your reality. The best way to identify what frequency you're on is through your emotions – your emotions show a true reflection of your energy. Sometimes we can believe we're in a positive state of mind or taking good actions, but deep down we know we're not; we're just pretending. If we pay attention to our emotions, we can see the true nature of our vibration and therefore what we're attracting into our life. If we feel good, we'll think good thoughts, and as a result we'll take positive actions.

Good Vibes Only

Good vibes are simply higher states of vibration.

The terms *good* and *positive* are used interchangeably to describe something desirable. For example, every time you label a past event as a good or positive experience, you're referring to it in this way because it went as you'd hoped – or at least not as badly as it could have.

Essentially, you want the things you want because they make you feel good. All of life's desires are pursued to bring about a pleasurable emotional state and to avoid displeasure. Most of us believe that attaining our desires will lead to happiness.

Given that emotion is one of the most powerful vibrations you can control, and, fundamentally, positive emotions are what we're in search of, we can infer that our quest in life is to experience good vibrations. Think about it: when you feel good, your life also appears to be good. If you could continuously experience good vibes, you'd always view your life in a positive light.

Physician Dr Hans Jenny is known for coining the term 'cymatics', which is the study of visible sound and vibration. One of his best-known experiments shows the effect of sound on sand sprinkled onto a flat metal plate that's made to vibrate at different frequencies by stroking a violin bow against its edge. Various patterns are formed depending on the different frequencies. At higher vibrations, beautifully intricate patterns are formed; lower vibrations produce less appealing shapes. A higher vibration, then, creates more enjoyable effects.

Ideally, we want to feel as loving and joyful as we can in life. These are the highest-vibrating feelings, and will help us manifest more of what we want – and, by extension, more good vibrations. In contrast, feelings of hatred, anger and despair have a very low vibration. They'll attract more of what we don't want.

Based on the principle of the Law of Vibration, to receive good vibes we must project good vibes. As transmitters and receivers of vibrational frequencies, the vibrations we put out are *always* pulling in stuff that's vibrating at a similar frequency to us. This means the feelings we put out into the Universe will be returned to us through matching vibrations. So, if you send out feelings of joy, then you'll be given more things to feel joyful about. The common

The feelings we project are returned on a like-for-like basis through our experiences.

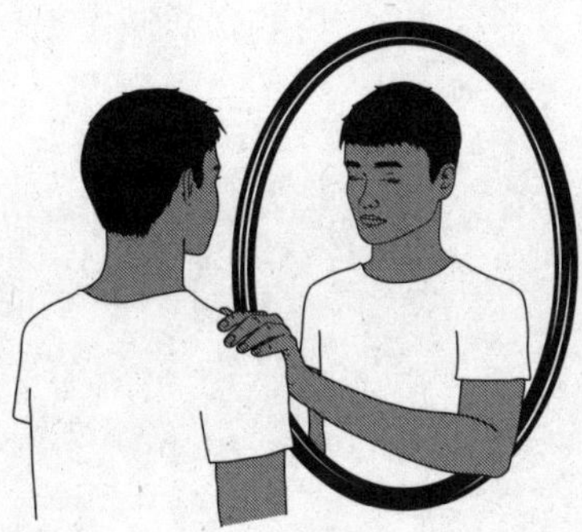

misconception is that you'll feel good only once you have what you want. The truth is that you can feel good *right now*.

Ultimately, self-love and raising the level of your vibration go hand in hand. When you make an effort to raise your vibration, you show yourself the love and care you deserve. You'll feel good and attract good. By taking positive actions and changing your mindset, you'll manifest greater things. By loving yourself, you'll live a life you love.

PART TWO

Positive Lifestyle Habits

Introduction

Higher states of vibration will help you feel good, which means you can manifest more good things in your life.

Your aim is to feel better by vibrating higher. There are many lifestyle habits that will help you do this and bring you closer to a more loving and joyful state.

You can change your emotional state through all sorts of activities that will raise your vibration, some of which will have a lasting effect while others may make you feel good only in the moment.

For example, if you feel upset because you've fallen out with a friend, you might be able to change your emotional state by doing something fun with other friends instead. Other ways you might raise your vibration include physical touch with a loved one, laughing, listening to uplifting music, spreading kindness, sleeping deeply, moving your body or engaging in any other activity you enjoy. But afterwards you might be left to face your misery again. Nothing has improved in your mind; you have just temporarily avoided the problem.

Alternatively, the practice of meditation can, over time, completely change the way your brain functions. Meditation and the introspective act of studying your low-vibration emotions can help you transform these to higher-vibration emotions. Thus, meditation might help you view the fall out with your friend in a more positive way. (We'll spend more time exploring meditation further on.)

Since everything is energy, you could say that everything you engage with will affect your vibration somehow. But new actions and changing your mindset in a positive way are also elements of self-love, to become the best – and happiest – person you can be.

There are also new actions we can take to make ourselves feel better that may seem to work only for a short while to begin with, but when carried out consistently over a long period of time become habits that reap lasting results.

Surround yourself with positive people

Surround yourself with people who are vibin' higher than you. Be around people who are feeling better than you are. Energy is contagious.

When you're not feeling too good, try being around people who are. They're vibrating higher than you and there's a good chance that you can absorb some of their energy. Just as the green alga *Chlamydomonas reinhardtii* has been found by researchers to draw energy from other plants,[5] my experience suggests that there's great potential for humans to do something very similar.

Have you ever met someone for the first time and felt like something isn't quite right about them? You can't quite put your

---

5 Blifernez-Klassen, O., Doebbe, A., Grimm, P., Kersting, K., Klassen, V., Kruse, O., Wobbe, L., 'Cellulose degradation and assimilation by the unicellular phototrophic eukaryote Chlamydomonas reinhardtii' (*Nature Communications*, November 2012)

finger on it but you just get a bad vibe, and usually you find out later on that there was a good reason for this feeling. Energy doesn't lie.

You've probably experienced the opposite, too. There are certain people who we identify as being full of positive energy. They always seem to infect those around them with their good vibes. I've changed my emotional state many times just by being around cheerful people.

Positive people can also provide empowering perspectives on our problems. Being in a positive state, they're more likely to have an optimistic outlook on what we're going through. They'll try to look for the positives in the situation and help us change our focus to something that lifts our vibe.

So, make a commitment to build meaningful and lasting relationships with positive people. When you spend more time with people who add value to your life and elevate your mood, you'll begin to adopt their encouraging thinking patterns and reflect their vibrations back at them.

The Law of Vibration suggests that we attract people who are vibrating on the same frequency as us. So, if we can begin to experience more positive emotions on a regular basis as a result of other people, we'll attract even more positive people into our life, thus reinforcing the good vibes around us.

Change your body language

It's hard to crack a smile when things are going wrong. But a 2003 study by Simone Schnall and James Laird showed that if you fake a smile, you can actually trick your brain into thinking you're happy by releasing feel-good hormones called endorphins.[6]

This might seem a little wacky at first. If smiling for no reason feels too strange, then find a reason to smile. You could smile at the prospect of your smile itself making someone else feel happier. They might smile back at you, giving you a genuine reason to keep your smile alive.

In fact, our entire body and physiology can affect our thoughts and feelings. By changing our outer state, we can change our inner

6 Schnall, S., Laird, J.D., 'Keep smiling: Enduring effects of facial expressions and postures on emotional experience and memory' (Clark University, Massachusetts, 2003)

state. It may also surprise you to learn that the vast majority of messages that we give other people are non-verbal, such as facial expressions, gestures or even the way we hold ourselves while we're talking. For this reason, it's important that we try to think about the messages we're conveying with our body language.

If I told you to show me how someone would appear if they were depressed, you'd probably know exactly how to portray them: you'd slump with your head down, looking grim. If I asked you to show me how someone would appear if they were angry, you could do that with ease, too.

Now think about how a person who is happy and feels high on life would appear. What would their facial expression be like? How would they be standing? Is there a particular way they'd be moving? Where might their hands be? Are they likely to be making any gestures? What tone would their voice take? How fast or slow would they be talking?

If you can act like someone who feels good, your internal state will change and your vibration will rise.

You might be concerned that this is an unhealthy way to raise your vibration. But the idea that you can 'fake it 'til you make it' has been proven many times. For example, Muhammad Ali famously said, 'To be a great champion, you must believe you are the best. If you're not, pretend you are.' Take Ali's fight with Sonny Liston: before the fight Ali was an underdog, but he chose to act like he was going to whop Liston – boasting and bragging about it to fans – and, in the fight, he did.

Social psychologist Amy Cuddy is renowned for her work on how body language not only affects how others see us, but also how we see ourselves. A report co-authored by Cuddy claims that simply by doing one of three poses related to power for only two minutes a day, you can create a 20 per cent increase in the confidence hormone testosterone and a 25 per cent decrease in the stress hormone, cortisol.[7] The so-called 'power poses' are a quick and easy way to feel more powerful, says the report.

Some people get the wrong end of the stick and pretend to have some particular asset or talent to seek attention from others so that they can feel better about themselves. But if you simply act

---

7 Carney, D., Cuddy, A., Yap, A., 'Power Posing: Brief Nonverbal Displays Affect Neuroendocrine Levels and Risk Tolerance' (*Psychological Science*, 2010)

a particular way to enhance your confidence and feel better about where you're going, it becomes a useful technique. This imagined confidence will then gradually start to become genuine confidence, and the closer you get to it through matching vibrations, the more genuine it becomes.

Take some time out

Don't underestimate the importance of taking time to relax. Sometimes, we get so caught up in our lives and what's going on around us that we become overwhelmed and tense.

The simple solution is to unwind and keep some distance from the things that are stressing you out. Don't be afraid to spend some time alone. I've noticed that sometimes you can feel *peopled out*. If you're an introvert, this feeling might be quite common. You feel like everyone wants a piece of you and it just gets too much.

If you're living with a spouse, friends or family, this might seem a little cruel. It's not that you dislike them, or that you're even fed up with them. It's just that you need a break: a chance to breathe and recharge. You just need to be alone for a while. That's perfectly acceptable and doesn't make you any less loving.

It's also easy to feel overstimulated by the media and social media, and in need of a period of rest from these things, too.

How can you tell if you need a break?

Well, here's an example. If someone tries to do something nice for you, yet you feel like they're trying too hard or they're all up in your space, it might be a sign that you're all peopled out. Yes, you might feel bad, because you know this person has good intentions. But you just want them to stop.

In Mexican Spanish, the word *engentado* describes this particular feeling. It refers to the feeling of wanting to be away from people after spending time with them.

Although you shouldn't let your mood dictate your manners, neither should you feel bad for wanting to disconnect for a bit. It's not only beneficial for you, but for others, too. The longer you stay peopled out without a recharge, the higher the chance that you'll lower other people's vibrations.

It's also very powerful to spend some time in nature. In this day and age, it's increasingly difficult to navigate through life without technology. However, being out in nature can help to replenish and rejuvenate your entire being. A research study published in

Sometimes you have to unplug yourself from the world for a moment, so you can reset yourself.

1991 found that natural environments had recuperative effects by bringing about positive emotional states and encouraging psychological wellbeing.[8]

You don't have to make this complicated. You could go outside for a walk, do some work in your garden, go and sit under a tree, or gaze up at the stars. If the sun is shining, absorbing some rays of light can help boost your vitamin D and levels of serotonin, a 'happy' hormone that acts as a natural mood stabilizer.

8 Fiorito, E., Losito, B., Miles, M., Simons, R., Ulrich, R., Zelson, M., 'Stress recovery during exposure to natural and urban environments' (*Journal of Environmental Psychology*, Volume 11, Issue 3, September 1991)

Find some inspiration

Inspiration keeps me driven and optimistic. Nowadays, there are so many ways that we can get inspired. Self-help books, newspapers or empowering novels like *The Alchemist* by Paulo Coelho are great, as are myriad digital sources of inspiration such as podcasts. Don't underestimate the power of a great inspirational movie, either. I personally find *The Pursuit of Happyness*, starring actor Will Smith, very uplifting.

I remember one particular period during which I felt completely lost in life. I'd just left a job to pursue my own business, selling inspirational T-shirts. I'd invested my own money, and to my dismay they weren't selling as well as I'd hoped. I thought they were going to be sold out within days. I'd read all these business textbooks, spent hours on fashion blogs and felt like I had all the knowledge required to run a successful company and bring something innovative to the fashion world. However, my reality was proving otherwise.

I was beginning to lose faith in myself and my abilities. I questioned my direction in life and, on top of this, my mum saw that I was struggling and told me I should get another job as I needed to make money to live on and help out at home. The pressure felt immense.

When you begin to doubt your abilities, you can quickly fall deep into a sea of misery. You begin to experience all the lower vibrational states and this can be damaging.

I knew I had to do something. So I listened to various personal development audiobooks, picked up some more self-help books, streamed online videos and read articles, quotes and blog posts. I even started speaking to entrepreneurial friends I'd met via social media.

I started learning about other people's hardships and how they overcame them, even when the odds were against them. I started to feel inspired and my self-belief grew. These stories were demonstrating that my failure wasn't final. Anyone who has accomplished anything great has faced big challenges or failures. But they're only *final* if you quit.

Admittedly, my T-shirt business didn't work out. But it sparked changes, ones that benefited me hugely. When you're inspired, you find drive and you feel good about where you're going and what's possible in your life.

Stay clear of gossip and drama

Drama is for TV, not for real life.
Don't play a part in someone else's episode
in which they are the only star.

At some point, everyone will find themselves taking part in gossip. Sometimes, they won't even realize that they're doing it. The worst part is that most people actually enjoy it; they don't think they're being judgemental and see gossiping as harmless. They just love the excitement of hearing juicy rumours about those around them and passing them on – then getting a reaction. And this makes gossiping a great way to lower your vibration!

Regardless, spreading gossip preys on our ego: we do it to try to feel good about ourselves; to feel superior to others. It's very often judgemental, and most judgements stem from hatred, which is a low vibrational state that will only lead to you inviting unpleasant experiences into your life.

As we've already established, every thought and word holds a powerful vibration. When we discuss others in a negative way, we're sending negative energy out into the Universe. As a result, this lowers our own vibration, resulting in toxic events in our lives that will reproduce ill feelings. *Ayurveda*, the ancient Indian medical system, says gossiping affects some of our energy centres, known as chakras. This actively restricts us from ascending to higher vibrational states.

News outlets profit from gossip by publicizing other people's misfortune. Luckily for them, some people buy into it. As a result, it's become socially acceptable to discuss other people. Yet everyone knows they wouldn't like it if *they* were the subject of gossip.

So, distance yourself from conversations about others, or try to direct the discussion to something more positive. You'll notice that, more often than not, people who spend their time gossiping are the ones who seem to complain or find comfort in misery. If you join them in their habits, you'll gradually become disillusioned with life, too.

Similarly, getting swept up in unnecessary drama can heighten both stress and anxiety. This puts you in a lower emotional state and, as you already know by now, this reflects undesirably on your life. Why give up your joy?

I've learned to avoid drama at all costs because it does nothing good for me. I once came across a high-drama person who attempted to argue with me about a point I'd made. Ironically, my point had been that we should walk away from fights because they can destruct our peace, but he didn't believe that we should. When I kindly told him that I respected our differences and we should move on, he got angry. If I'd felt he was actually interested in my perspective, I'd have been happy to share it and listen to his. However, he only wanted to argue, to prove me wrong and drag me down.

His ears were shut and his mouth was open: he wasn't ready to learn, only to dictate. Our beliefs were different and he got really worked up by it. To him, I was spreading false information and creating further suffering in the world with my viewpoint. This anger was followed by personal abuse directed towards me, particularly since I wouldn't take part in his battle. I simply stayed silent and observed until I could distance myself.

It didn't seem like this person cared deeply for other people's wellbeing, or that he wanted to prevent suffering in the world. His aggressive behaviour contradicted his points. He simply needed to justify why he was right and that his way was the only way. My beliefs shattered his truth that we should always fight back, and without that truth, his identity became threatened.

This is the work of the ego. Your ego is your self-image created by thought. It's your social mask, one that constantly requires validation because it lives in fear of losing its sense of identity. When you're upset because someone doesn't like you, it's your ego operating: you validate your existence based on their approval. When they disapprove of you, you no longer feel good about who you are.

Our ego always wants to feel significant and adored. It seeks instant gratification. It wants to feel more powerful than other people.

It's the reason people buy things they don't need – to impress people they don't even care about. It's the reason we become bitter about other people's successes. It's the reason greed exists and why we're constantly striving to outdo others. It prevents us from acting with love and understanding.

Unfortunately, many of us identify ourselves with a certain image throughout our lives that's created by our ego, and we have to keep on maintaining and protecting it. If others don't approve of the image of ourselves that we've created, our identity becomes threatened and the ego will fear for its protection, just as in the case here. My beliefs forced that person to question his own beliefs and therefore question his identity, which posed a threat. This is why he was so quick to get defensive and to attack.

This happens a lot in life because of ego. People don't say or ask things out of curiosity; they simply want to prove others wrong. They want people to follow their truth, not because they necessarily care about others, but because they fear being wrong and not knowing who they are. There are a lot of high-drama people in the world who seem to thrive in these toxic conditions.

I try to keep an open mind and to listen to other people's perspectives. However, I've also learned not to waste time on people who have no interest in what I have to say, or why I say it. You must make sure that you don't involuntarily take part in the internal battles of others.

Discussing problems and sharing information is fine when the intention doesn't stem from the desire to make yourself feel superior through the belittlement of others. This provides a false sense of self and consequently lowers your vibe. There are better ways to spend your time than gossiping or involving yourself in dramas. Instead, try to focus on your own life and on trying to improve it. Time is precious and you should be investing it wisely by doing something constructive that will make your life greater.

Sort out your nutrition and water

What you consume, consumes you; what consumes you, controls your life.

Everything you eat and drink is important, as it affects your vibration and reality. Think about it: how can you feel good if you don't ingest good foods and good fluids?

The foods that leave us feeling sleepy and sluggish are those that vibrate at a lower frequency. Hence, when we eat them, our vibration also changes. A lot of these foods are junk foods – and, unfortunately, they're engineered to taste great. For this reason, some of us tend to overindulge in the bad stuff, and it doesn't just dampen our mood but also adds on extra pounds and makes us vulnerable to illness.

In 1949, a French electromagnetism expert called André Simoneton published his research on the electromagnetic waves of particular foods. He realized that each food not only has a particular amount of calories (chemical energy), but also an electromagnetic power that's vibrational.[9]

Simoneton discovered that humans must maintain a vibration of 6500 angstroms for them to be deemed healthy (an angstrom is a unit measuring 100 millionth of a centimetre, used to express the size of electromagnetic wavelengths).

Simoneton divided the foods into four categories, according to a scale of zero to 10,000 angstroms.

The first category was full of high-vibration foods, including fresh fruits and raw vegetables, wholegrains, olives, almonds, hazelnuts, sunflower seeds, soy and coconut.

The second category had lower-vibration foods, such as boiled vegetables, milk, butter, eggs, honey, cooked fish, peanut oil, sugar cane and wine.

The third category consisted of foods with very low vibrations, among them cooked meats, sausages, coffee and tea, chocolate, jams, processed cheeses and white bread.

---

9 Simoneton, A., *Radiations des aliments, ondes humaines et santé* (Le Courrier du Livre, 1971)

The fourth and final category exhibited practically no angstroms and included margarine, conserves, alcoholic spirits, refined white sugar and bleached flour.

Simoneton's research provides us with insight into which foods are good for our vibration and which ones we should avoid.

In addition, as a general rule, good-quality organic produce, as intended by nature, will keep you feeling more vitalized than non-organic foods. The price of organic food can be high but the expense may turn out to be less of a sacrifice than your health, if this deteriorates due to eating unhealthy foods.

We should also consider the importance of water. It's estimated that around 60–70 per cent of your whole body is composed of water, and it's essential to your body's functioning: it keeps you hydrated and flushes away unwanted toxins, and this will keep you at a higher vibrational state. If the water balance in your body falls below the necessary amount, your body will react adversely. You may be unable to focus, feel dizzy and even become unconscious.

Simoneton's research showed alcoholic spirits to be very low-vibration, and regular consumption of excessive amounts can be very harmful and even cause death through liver damage. Too much alcohol also creates false perception, which may lead you to behave in a way you normally wouldn't – this can lead to bad choices that might be damaging to your life. Alcohol might provide a few moments of pleasure, but you must moderate how much of it you consume.

Make fresh, filtered water your primary source of fluid.

Express gratitude

Before you complain about school, remember that some people can't even get an education.

Before you complain about getting fat, remember that some people don't even have any food.

Before you complain about your job, remember that some people don't even have any money.

Before you complain about cleaning the house, remember that some people don't even have any shelter.

Before you complain about washing the dishes, remember that some people don't even have any water.

Before you complain about all these things on social media using your smartphone, without any consideration of how blessed you are, just be thankful for a minute.

Being thankful is one of the simplest, and yet most powerful, habits you can cultivate. By counting your blessings daily, you can begin to condition your mind to look for the good in everything around you. Soon enough, you'll unconsciously begin to see the bright side of things and feel better about life.

You can't feel *bad* while you're feeling thankful. As simple as showing gratitude sounds, most people struggle with it. It's much easier to focus on burdens than on gifts; to devote your attention to the things you don't have, rather than the things you do have.

I was once studying some of the most successful individuals on this planet, and one phrase really stuck with me: 'Greatness starts with being grateful'. I didn't think too much of it at the time, but as I've grown older I've begun to understand its value. I've realized that you can't feel joy without being thankful; being thankful is a vital component of happiness.

Furthermore, by expressing gratitude, we not only transform our vibrational state to become more magnetic to the good things, but we also become able to put things into perspective. We go through each day constantly comparing ourselves to others, and most of us rarely acknowledge that *we* have what others may desire. We also tend to compare ourselves to those we consider more fortunate than us, rather than those who are less fortunate. Just think of the amount of people who have to live through war on a daily basis. But we're completely safe from such troubles, and many more that we hear about in the news.

It's easy to say 'thanks' without really meaning it. The key to showing gratitude is to *feel* thankful. I'll use my coaching client Will as an example to illustrate how you can reach a true state of gratitude.

After Will had started by reeling off a list of all of his problems, I asked him to tell me what he was thankful for. His response was that he couldn't think of anything!

I knew his car meant a lot to him, so I asked, 'How about your car?'

He replied, 'Yeah, I'm thankful for my car, I guess.' This level of gratitude is a nice start, but it doesn't really change our state.

Then I asked Will what it would mean if he didn't have his car. He sat there for a moment and thought about it. Then he began to list things: 'I wouldn't be able to go to work, pick up the groceries, go and see my friends... and I wouldn't be able to pick up my kids from school.'

I could see his state changing as he started naming these things and envisioning them in his mind. I then went a step further and asked, 'What would it mean if you weren't able to pick up your kids?'

He replied, 'Well, they'd have to walk back home or take the bus.'

I pressed, 'And how would that walk back be for them?'

Suddenly, he imagined them walking back in the cold weather. Will knew they'd be unsafe. And he was visibly unsettled.

After a few moments, he thought back to when he was a kid and how he used to get bullied on the bus home. This was when it hit him. He took a heavy breath. I could see the relief on his face as he thought back to his car. He finally admitted how grateful he was that he not only had a car, but also that it helped him improve the lives of those he loved. His state completely transformed and I observed the shift in his body language.

When practising gratitude, imagine how different your life would be without that particular thing you're showing thanks for. It will produce strong feelings and emotions. And *this* is how you can get into a powerful state of gratitude.

Remember, there might be many things in your world that are going wrong. Yet there are also many things that are going right.

> *The more you count your blessings, the more blessings you'll have to count.*

Here's a short story. During my time working in an office, I had a manager who I didn't see eye to eye with, and we both made work difficult for each other. However, as he had more authority, he always had the upper hand.

For months I let his actions affect my mood and therefore how I acted. I reacted with resentment, I gossiped about him, I hated going into work and I continued to emit all these negative thoughts and feelings out into the Universe. As a result, things just got worse – *much worse!*

I wanted to distance myself from him, but he sat right beside me, so I couldn't. Even when I did manage to get away from him, he'd find a way to provoke me. Back then, I wasn't afraid to vocalize how I felt, even if it was going to sound sour. I had no problem telling him he had no leadership qualities, which obviously didn't make things any better.

After viewing some online videos from spiritual teacher Esther Hicks, I realized that I was utilizing my energy in the wrong way. I was aware that the problem was there, but I was feeding the problem rather than focusing on a solution – once I started to do that, things started to get better.

I made a conscious effort to show gratitude for having a job that paid well. I knew how difficult it was just to find a job, but especially one with a generous salary; my salary enabled me to enjoy many comforts in life. I regularly reminded myself of these things to ensure I was in a state of appreciation – a high vibrational state.

A few months later, my manager was promoted to another team. I also got a pay rise while experiencing much more freedom at work. This period was among my favourite in this job. Simply because I'd decided to feel good, I was given rewards that made me feel even better!

Too many of us direct our energy towards our fears. I'm not saying your problems don't exist, but try instead to focus your energy on solutions to those problems. The Universe is abundant in all areas; the illusion of fear is the only limitation we have.

Study your emotions

Ignoring negative emotions is like keeping poison in your system. Learn to understand everything that you feel. The aim isn't to force positive thoughts, but to transform the negative ones into something healthier, so you can feel better.

Our dominant thoughts significantly influence our emotions; they're crucial to how we feel. The issue many of us have when we try to become positive thinkers is that we ignore the transformation process. We assume that it's better to wipe out negative thoughts, numb our feelings and move on to more positive ideas. This is often ineffective because you're just trying to trick yourself into thinking things are okay, when your true feelings suggest otherwise. Repressed feelings can become toxic within your system and can eventually cause damage.

If a venomous thought sits deep within your mind, it will reappear when you experience a similar situation in the future. Not only will this lower your vibration, but the continuity of this pattern can also damage your mental health, and in turn your physical health. You may also become extremely toxic for others to be around, making you lonely and further adding to your misery.

So don't suppress your negative emotions. Instead, transform them so you can raise your vibration – not just now, but for all similar events in the future. Understanding your emotions will allow you to transform them from a low vibration to a high vibration over and over again. This is why introspection is so important to personal development.

For example, a client of mine called Sarah had started talking to a new love interest. A few days into messaging and calling each other, he went quiet. She waited by her phone, expecting him to text her back, but he didn't. As a result, the dominant thought in her head said, 'No one is interested in me or has time for me because I'm ugly.' This made her feel sad.

Sarah needed to turn her negative emotions back into positive ones, so we followed my step-by-step method for achieving this.

How to transform negative emotions

1. **Identify:** to change your emotional state, you must identify what emotion you're feeling. In Sarah's example, she felt sad and afraid. After delving deeper, we identified that Sarah also felt neglected and insecure.

2. **Challenge:** the next step would be to question yourself: Why do you feel the way you do? What thoughts are responsible for this?

   Sarah felt sad because she didn't get a text back. The thought that played back to her was that no one had time for her or was interested in her because she was ugly. This made her feel lonely and insecure.

   At this stage, you have consciously begun to observe your thoughts. A lot of the beliefs we have are based on exaggeration, misconception and opinions imposed on us by other people. Therefore, we can challenge these erroneous ideas and judgements in our mind. We can analyse our thought processes and change our negative thought patterns to more positive ones, in a logical way.

   Begin to challenge the beliefs behind your thoughts by questioning their validity. For example, Sarah asked herself:

Is it true that no one has time for me because I'm ugly? In thinking deeply about this question, Sarah began to learn a lot about why she felt the way she did. At this stage, you can ask questions that force you to dig deeper. You can also ask extreme questions, because they'll inspire extreme answers. In our example, Sarah went on to ask herself: Does this mean I'll never be happy?

Sarah pondered on these questions and saw that she was exaggerating the situation. One man failing to text her back didn't mean that she'd never be happy. She was reminded that her joy wasn't dependent on how others interacted with her.

Posing questions to yourself can reveal limitations in your thinking, as they did for Sarah. You'll begin to realize that you have made false assumptions and focused on the negative aspects of situations in your life.

Try it. Perhaps bring up a past experience that made you unhappy, and ask yourself direct questions that help you get to the heart of the matter. It's important to realize that we create our own sadness by attaching negative conclusions to these past experiences in our subconscious mind. Here we must challenge these conclusions, which are stored as lessons. Failing to correct the negative lessons means they're replayed in your subconscious mind. Over time, these lessons on repeat can weigh you down and induce depression.

3. **Understand:** This step is all about appreciating the deeper meaning behind the emotion. In our example, Sarah found that she was feeling insecure as a result of her recent experience. She started to worry that she wasn't good enough. During the days when her love interest *was* texting back, she felt better about herself. It was clear that she had a high need for social acceptance and approval.

   You must recognize the deeper meanings behind your feelings and make use of them as opportunities to grow. Sarah determined her worth based on what others thought because she had low self-esteem. She needed to be valued and accepted to feel better about herself.

4. **Replace:** These disempowering thoughts must then be replaced with empowering ones. You must ask yourself: How can I view or do things differently, to help myself feel better and live a greater life?

It's essential to transform destructive thoughts into ones that make you feel better in the moment. Sarah reminded herself that she was worthy of love, regardless of how others might behave towards her. She said, 'I love myself and that is enough. The love I give myself will be given back to me by someone who truly cares about me.'

To add substance to these empowering thoughts, think back to times when you truly felt the way you want to feel. Sarah came up with a memory in which she felt worthy, confident and loved. She held this scene in her head and relived the moment.

This technique not only boosts confidence, but it may also bring forth a solution. You may remember something you did during a similar situation in the past that helped you to manage it.

5. **Visualize:** Visualize yourself handling the emotion you're currently feeling – in the future. As you do this, not only will your vibration increase, but you'll also begin to create an autonomous association with that emotion that'll enable your brain to handle it for you effortlessly down the line.

   You can do this over and over again, each time stretching your imagination and making it more real in your mind's eye.

Repetition is the key to mastery. If you rehearse over and over again a situation in which you deal with the emotion, you'll know exactly how to manage it next time it comes up in your life.

Awareness of the present

Every second you spend thinking about the next moment you avoid embracing the present. Ensure your life isn't lived entirely in your head.

With global advances in technology, our society is becoming more engrossed in personal gadgets than in the world around them. We hold our phones more than we hold real conversations, and each other. We're so busy looking down at screens and engaging in digital interactions that we forget about the environment around us.

It seems people would rather experience an event through a camera than use their eyes to enjoy what's in front of them. Concert audiences are lit up by the shimmering of phone screens. This isn't to say that we shouldn't capture mementos of these precious times. But living through a screen prevents us from being present in the moment.

As we continue to distract ourselves from the present moment, we become more anxious, fearful and stressed. Worries overwhelm us in our everyday lives because we're now conditioned to live elsewhere, rather than right here. What's more, we ignore the people around us and our personal relationships pay the price.

This is often why we feel distressed, disconnected and lost. Our vibration is lowered because we feel like we're in some imagined situation that doesn't match up with our lived reality. We relive moments of the past, fear the future and create obstacles in our minds. We devote creative energy to destructive ideas – and this invites turmoil into our lives.

Now is the only time you have. Once your past is gone, it doesn't exist, no matter how many times you recreate it mentally. The future hasn't even arrived; but again, you keep taking yourself there mentally. Tomorrow comes disguised as today and some of us don't even notice. Nothing is more valuable than the present moment because you can never get it back. You may create a visual memory that you can retrace, but physically you cannot experience it again.

Think about a time when you completely forgot to check the clock or look at your phone. Perhaps you were around the people you

Technology is a tool,
not a substitute for living.

love, or doing something you enjoy. You were so engrossed in the moment that you had no time to worry about the past or the future. You were simply enjoying where you were. This is what's known as being in the present moment.

As we'll explore later in this book, planning for the future is vital in order to meet your goals, but we shouldn't spend too much time there. When you think about it, the present is still the future, disguised as now. Ten years ago you may have considered the future to be this exact point in your life. The future is today.

In my early twenties, if I knew I was going out on a Saturday night, I'd want every other day to hurry up. I was wishing away my precious time – time I'd never get back. Once Saturday arrived, and then passed, I moved on to focus on another day on which I was planning something exciting... and sometimes that was weeks away!

This is also the premise of life. Once we're born, every 24 hours we're moving one day closer towards our death. The future we're constantly waiting for arrives only as the present. Once it arrives, it passes by so quickly we don't even notice. We quickly switch our attention to anticipating the next moment, and then the next, and on and on.

This is how most of us live. We wake up to get through the day and then go back to sleep. We do this 365 times a year. We wait for success, love, happiness to show up, never really aware of what we have in the present moment. Eventually, we realize that we've never really lived. Or we finally have the riches we wanted yet we can't enjoy them because there's always something else to achieve.

We make life all about a future that exists only in our imagination and completely miss what's happening in front of us.

We could say the same about the past. Although we might have fond memories that we enjoy revisiting every now and again, we must learn to accept that once the past is gone, it cannot be changed. We can only reconstruct or alter it in our minds.

The meditation exercise that I'll discuss next can help you connect to the present. By developing awareness of the present moment, we can maintain a higher vibration because we avoid being paralysed by past pain or future fear.

Meditate

Meditation is growing in popularity and receiving praise from all directions: from occupational therapists to mainstream media, people from myriad different backgrounds are talking about the benefits of meditative work. But to the uninitiated, meditation practice can appear daunting, time-consuming and difficult to get to grips with. I personally avoided it for many years for these exact reasons.

Like many people, I planned to meditate but never quite got round to it. When I finally began, I found it awkward and wasn't sure if I was doing it right, or if it was working. My practice was inconsistent and I struggled to see how it could be of benefit to me. Once I looked deeper into it, however, I realized that I hadn't understood meditation as well as I'd thought. I'd overcomplicated it.

Once I committed myself to
30 consecutive days of focused meditation,
I began to feel a difference.

After a year of practising for 15 minutes a day, I noticed *incredible* changes within myself. Significantly, I found myself feeling angry far less often – something that had troubled me in the past. My rage was absent during situations identical to earlier events that had provoked an intense emotional response.

I also noticed a new ability to remain calm and at peace in the midst of chaos. I had more conscious control over my thoughts. As a result, I felt more joyful more often.

I couldn't ignore these changes.

Meditation eases the resistance that your ego creates. This brings a sense of calm, clarity and enhanced patience. I learn profound lessons from intuitive thoughts during my practice, and this access to my inner wisdom illuminates answers to any questions I've been struggling with. When I need to raise my vibration, I know that meditation will restore good feelings.

This might seem strange. Many people think the goal of meditation is to clear the mind of thoughts. But this is a misconception: actually, meditation is really *concentration*. Meditation helps you arrive at conscious awareness of the present moment – and that's a powerful tool to use in every part of your life.

You practise meditation by being fully present in the moment via your senses, while calmly observing your thoughts, emotions and bodily sensations – from a distance, without judgement.

I'd like to take you through a short relaxation meditation that you can do right now. You just need a pen, some paper and a quiet moment.

Meditate now – a step-by-step guide

1. Use your intuition to assess your level of energy. How would you rate your vibration level from one to 10, if one is *I feel low and I don't want to do anything*, and 10 is *I feel great, peaceful and full of joy*. Write down the first number that pops into your head – and don't question it.

2. Now we'll begin to move to a meditative state. Find somewhere you can completely relax, sitting or standing, with your eyes

open at this stage. Wherever you are, become aware of your body.

Are you sitting?

Are you standing?

How does your spine feel?

Don't change anything. Just become conscious of your physical body.

3. Now become conscious of your breathing. Just observe. Let the air go deep into your lungs, and then breathe out. Now, as you take a deep breath, imagine you're filling your lungs with as much air as possible, then expelling all the stale air as you exhale.

   Feel your belly moving up and down with every breath. Feel your chest move up and down with every breath.

4. Now look around you. Notice the colours and the patterns you see, without judgement. Just observe. Let your eyes absorb all that's around you. And then slowly close your eyes.

   Watch what comes to the screen of your mind.

Let your thoughts pass by, no pressure. There's no right or wrong. Relax your eyelids while you observe what comes and goes within your mind. And keep noticing the pattern of your breath: in, out; expansion and contraction.

5. Listen to the sounds around you.

   Where do they come from?

   What are the tones?

   Are there any sounds that stand out?

   Can you distinguish between background and foreground sounds?

   And now you can listen to the sound of your breath. In and out.

6. Bring your awareness to your entire body. Is there any tension? There's no need to change anything. Simply notice any sensations in your body.

   Are there any feelings or emotions arising right now? What are they? Where in your body are they located?

   Observe, feel and listen. Stay still for the next minute. When you're ready, slowly start to move your hands and feet.

   And then open your eyes.

7. This is the end of the exercise, so let's check your level of energetic vibration. How would you rate your vibration level now? Write down your number. Is it higher than before? If not, you can do the exercise again. Eventually you'll find that this brief practice raises your vibration.

If you struggle to remember the steps above, try recording them on your phone so that your voice can guide you through them. Speak slowly and clearly, and allow pauses for silence while you read the instructions.

Meditation is far from being complicated. Buddhist master Yongey Mingyur Rinpoche claims that to meditate you need only to be aware of your breath:[10] when you breathe with awareness, you're meditating. It's as simple as that – and that's why you can meditate anywhere, at any time.

Everything and anything done in a state of conscious awareness can be meditation – even the washing-up.

---

10 'Learn meditation from this Buddhist monk' (MBS Fitness, YouTube, 2016)

Try it for 15 minutes a day, for 30 consecutive days. If that seems too much, start with five minutes and build up gradually.

Breathing is such an important part of our life. I mean, really – if we don't breathe, we don't live. We inhale and life starts, and as life ends, we exhale. That's why it's said that with every breath there's transformation occurring within us. We die and are reborn with every breath that we take.

It's through breath that we reinforce our vital force, our life energy – often referred to as *mana*, *prana*, *chi* or *ki*, among numerous other names, depending on the spiritual tradition. With each breath, we're allowing life force energy to enter every cell of our body so it can vibrate with new life. As we take fuller and more controlled breaths, this enables our nervous system to calm us down, increasing our vibration.

Meditation breaks down the walls of our conditioned mind and gives us an opportunity to become more authentic. As you meditate more often, you'll gain perspective on the restricting thoughts you've been playing over in your mind.

PART THREE

Make Yourself a Priority

Introduction

It's not selfish or a sign of weakness to distance yourself or walk away from those who constantly bring down your vibe. Life is about balance. It's about spreading kindness, but it's also about not letting anyone take that kindness away from you.

Do you think it's selfish to put yourself first? Depending on the context, it *can* be selfish to think of yourself and not others. For example, if a pie is cut into eight equal pieces and there are eight hungry people in the room, it would be selfish of you to take two pieces.

However, it's often important to put yourself first. You have a lot of energy to give, but you must save some of that energy for yourself. You came into this world alone and you'll leave on your own. Your longest relationship in life is with yourself. Only when you manage this relationship well can you manage your relationships with others.

Sadly, we must accept that even though someone means well, they may repeatedly inflict pain on our souls without considering the effect that their actions and words are having on us. Ideally, we want to be in a place where our mood doesn't shift because of someone else's behaviour, but only the most spiritually evolved among us are able to do this – to demonstrate unconditional, ongoing love in spite of others' actions towards them. Most of us still have a long way to go before we ascend into states of consciousness high enough to allow us to love all people without condition or expectation.

If we're not spiritually evolved individuals, then constant interaction with toxic people can suck the energy out of us, which in time will make us feel drained.

It is much easier to see the good in life
when you are around positive people.

Your personal growth is an ongoing process and it can take a long time to get to a place where you're unaffected by other people's behaviour.

So sometimes you have to cut out those people who continuously cut you. They're venomous and restrict your progress. After all, it's hard to function, not to mention crack a smile, when someone keeps feeding you poison. Think of a plant: if you keep it under toxic conditions, it can't grow and will soon start to wither. But, under the right conditions, it'll thrive and grow into something beautiful. Once it becomes big and strong, it's hard to destroy.

People can be toxic, too. A toxic person might be someone who criticizes everything you do; expects too much; lacks respect; shows very little support. They might ridicule, neglect, physically abuse, manipulate and belittle you. These people are usually unwilling to confront their toxic actions and make changes.

So when you find yourself around people who are toxic towards you, your inner peace will be lost and you'll be more likely to pass on the pain this causes you to others. This begs the question: Is it selfish to think of ourselves here, or is it selfish of them to expect that we should be okay with it?

Ending a toxic relationship can be incredibly difficult; it's hard to break free from those close to you, even if they're hurting you. But once you remove those people from your life, you make way for a river of positivity to flow. You'll have time and space for introspection, healing and growth, and like the plant, you too will become strong.

Check your own behaviour

We want everyone else to stop being toxic, but we rarely review our own actions. The most important relationship you have is the one with yourself, so there's no excuse not to break free from your own toxic ways. So it's important that you can identify any toxic tendencies you might have and that are hurting others – or yourself.

When we're annoyed or upset, we assume that everyone around us is fine. We excuse ourselves for acting in unkind ways by blaming our mood, not realizing that other people might be going through a tough time themselves. This can bring other people down, which means that not only are *you* feeling hurt, but now someone else is, too.

Even those who believe they're leading by example often forget to review their own actions, as demonstrated by an experience I've had myself. If you've seen my Instagram page, you'll know I post

Always review your behaviours and make an effort to change any that are toxic – towards yourself or others. This isn't only how you grow, it's also an act of self-love. You're showing yourself that you deserve better than the behaviours limiting your progress.

quotes and advice. What you might not know is that quite often my words are lifted by other social media pages and reposted as someone else's inspiring words. As flattering as it is to see my words and thoughts being shared by people, it's not satisfying seeing my watermark being removed and no credit given to me.

What really strikes me is that there are a number of pages promoting positivity to huge audiences that have still refused to correct their mistake. When I reached out, the people behind these pages told me they didn't want to take posts down and repost them correctly because they had great engagement on them and they'd lose followers. Some of these people had profited from my words but still didn't feel the need to acknowledge my messages. One said that everyone else was doing it, so I should get over it. Among the most interesting responses was: 'Let it go – your name doesn't need to be on it. If you're a positive person, then you don't need to contact me ever again.' This has led me to realize that even those who are doing the most preaching, and appearing to promote positivity and love, aren't always following their own advice.

In truth, I did need to get over it once they refused to do anything about it. I had to focus on working selflessly. I've managed to overcome my disappointment and remind myself that the most important thing for me is that a positive message is getting out there. This is how I find my peace.

However, this response exposed something that's very common in the world: shifting blame. We're quick to point out what's wrong with someone else so that we can avoid taking responsibility for our own actions.

We could say that it's not our responsibility if others are offended by our actions. After all, it's only their perception and ideas around our actions that are actually hurting them.

If I feel that I'm right, yet someone else feels that I'm wrong, who is right?

But even when you think someone's overreacting, you must try to understand the root cause of why they feel the way they do. Usually it's because you've violated one of their personal values. And if someone says they're hurt by your actions, you must believe they're hurt; you can't decide for them whether or not they felt hurt in the first place.

I've learned this with my partner. Sometimes I take my jokes too far and cause offence. If she then bravely admits her vulnerability to me, the worst thing I can do is make her feel bad for opening up to me by being defensive and shifting blame onto her. You can't tell someone that their feelings are invalid. You have to try to seek understanding first. Identify why they feel the way they do and then see what you can do to make it better.

This is important for all relationships. We're all different and we all deserve respect for our feelings. Acknowledging and understanding someone's pain not only allows you to learn about them, but also helps you to grow. You're not expected to be flawless. We all make mistakes. But you must be willing to learn, grow and remain respectful.

The power of a good partner

Create a relationship where you talk to each other about your problems, not where you talk about each other on social media. Statuses don't fix relationship issues, honest conversations do.

Sometimes in relationships, one partner will punish the other due to their own insecurities. They make the other feel like they have flaws, just to cover up their own limitations and to achieve a sense of superiority or authority. These relationships are often very unhealthy and toxic. They can make the one being punished question themselves and feel low or empty inside.

For example, if you think your nose is too big and then you notice your partner being friendly with someone who you perceive as being attractive, you may notice their nose is smaller and draw a comparison. As you focus on the idea that their nose is better than yours, you may feel a rush of negative emotions such as jealousy, doubt and hatred. As a result, your self-worth, confidence, and even energy, decreases.

Your mind may also suggest hideous ideas to you, such as your partner finding them attractive because their nose is *perfect*. You may then take your pain out on your partner, accusing them of flirting, even if it was completely innocent. You'll project your insecurity onto them and imply that they're malicious, they lack love and they're disrespectful. This is emotional manipulation, where instead of taking responsibility for your own emotions, you take them out on someone else.

You'll ensure your partner also feels your pain. You'll question their integrity and morals, trying to convince them that they're sinister. You'll point out everything that's wrong with them. This only leads to conflict, where even more insecurities may be exposed, damaging words exchanged and potentially devastating actions produced. But you need to understand where your actions are coming from. Is it your insecurities, or because your partner has been acting in toxic ways? Ultimately, this ends in pain.

Alternatively, your partner may have been genuinely flirting. In some relationships, this may be acceptable. In most, however, it won't be. Although you can't demand respect from someone, you can extract yourself from situations in which you're not respected.

That said, there are plenty of healthy relationships that are full of insecurities. But they must contain mutual respect and support. Partners should be honest about their insecurities, open to working with each other to improve them and respectful enough not to hurt the other or use their insecurities against them. All relationships require work. They require endless communication and tremendous understanding, and they can be very challenging. But while giving up isn't always the answer, sometimes you have to walk away, especially when you lose your sense of self.

Sometimes you have to break away from the toxicity so you can heal.

Unhealthy relationships drain all the goodness out of us. We give everything to someone who just won't match our efforts and willingness to try. We empty our love bank to make them feel wealthier, while we become broke. We give ourselves up to someone who doesn't respect us enough to treat us well in return.

You don't have to be an expert to realize that relationships should be empowering. They shouldn't consistently make you feel limited or lacking. You should never be feeling empty in a relationship, especially if it's to make someone else feel full.

Sometimes, we love the idea of what someone could be, or what someone is momentarily; we love their potential. In fact, if you reflect on your past with a serious ex-partner, there was probably a point where you thought that they were the best thing ever. Later, you may have found out that they weren't quite what you expected them to be.

None of us is perfect, so no relationship is perfect. But it's easy to fall into the trap of hanging on to people because you see their light and their potential to be a great partner; however, deep down you know that you're clinging to false hope. If you're with someone who isn't willing to get better, you may be wasting your time.

You can't change those who aren't ready to change.

You also have to ensure that they're not pretending they want to get better. This tactic could be used to build false hope, so that you stick around for longer. Of course, this is a selfish act and it's characteristic of someone who's unwilling to reach their full potential.

I completely understand that it might be painful to leave a toxic person who you love; getting out of a toxic relationship is much easier said than done. That's why many stay put and entertain the negativity for as long as they can. But you're worth that temporary pain.

Sometimes, people will settle for inadequate relationships because they believe they won't find someone better, or that the task of finding someone new and rebuilding something from scratch is too long and difficult. Their intuition will tell them that they deserve better but they won't courageously act on it.

Here's an example that might help you figure out whether you're in a toxic relationship. Someone once asked for my opinion on their relationship. They were having problems with their partner and didn't know if they should walk away. I don't like telling people what they should do in their relationship because I'm not in it and can't see the full picture. Someone can describe it to me and I can make assumptions, but the choice is ultimately theirs.

So I flipped it around and asked this person what they'd advise their daughter to do if she were in the same position. This gave them pause for thought. I already knew what they thought they should be doing – but they needed me either to justify it or talk them out of it. The decision scared them, so they were avoiding it. Yet when I asked this question, they realized they already knew the answer.

As a parent, you have natural protective instincts over your child. Even if you don't have a child, you can probably imagine it. You'd care about them so much that you wouldn't want them to get hurt and miss out on any joy. This person's gut already had the answer, even before they asked me for my advice. I always tell people to trust their instinct, because that's their soul whispering advice to them.

You'll know it's your gut when you have a sense of almost knowing *you've arrived at the answer without a reasoning process.*

When you think a certain thought, you'll get a strange little feeling in your belly, and that's what I believe is your intuition. It's one of the best guidance systems around!

Even your most dominant thoughts aren't necessarily your intuition speaking, because they could be rooted in fear or desire. Intuition is a calm feeling and gives you a reassuring sense of detachment. Sometimes, it will feel like something inside you is urging you to take note. It's almost physical.

Just remember, a relationship should add value to your life and bring you good vibes the majority of the time. Relationships that are toxic will deflate your psychological health and even your physical wellbeing.

Don't be in a relationship for the sake of being in one. If it's time to say goodbye, be brave and do it. It might hurt now, but it will be the source of something greater in the future.

Choose real friendships

One evening, I received an email from a teenager who'd diagnosed herself with depression and low self-esteem. She didn't feel good about life. She didn't feel confident and found it very hard to remain positive. Telling her to stay positive didn't work; it just made her feel worse.

After speaking to the teenager, it became obvious that her friends had put many disturbing ideas into her head, telling her she was ugly, stupid, embarrassing to be around. These friends didn't recognize her worth, and this affected how she saw herself, too.

If someone doesn't respect you or says you have flaws, there's a good chance you'll start to integrate their opinions into your sense of self. In fact, many of the thoughts in our heads aren't originally our own. When we're young, we might be told that we're not meant for certain paths in life. We grow up believing what we're told and the others' perceptions become our reality.

Our whole lives are shaped by throwaway comments and social programming.

Sometimes, the simplest solution is to be around different people, especially when you can't get the ones you're already surrounded by to change. Once the teenager let go of the friends she had and made new ones, she began to feel more confident about her life.

> *Simplify your circle of friends. Keep those who add value to your life; remove those who don't. Less is always more when your less* means *more.*

Since the evolution of social networking platforms, the definition of *friend* has changed. They're no longer people you know well. Virtual friendships have affected the way society labels friendships. We now call anyone a friend – even a person we met once on a night out.

How many of these people are really your friends? Could you turn to them in a time of need? Unfortunately, many modern friendships aren't based on emotional support or a family-like connection. Instead, they're based on drinking, smoking, partying, shopping or gossiping together – some of which happen to be habits that will lower your vibration.

A lot of these types of friendships may be based on short-term mutual gain. For example, some friends may only play an active role in your life when both of you need someone to accompany you to public events, such as parties. The person you go to the gym with might be considered a friend, but if you ever needed help moving house, would they be available to lend a hand? Would they offer to help? Although these friendships may not be bad, because they assist you in serving a purpose, they quickly fall away when you're in need of help. You can't always expect those people to be there for you.

Sometimes, we have more superficial friendships than meaningful ones. Consider whether your friends show you support. Do they applaud when you win? Do they encourage you to take positive actions? Do they help you grow as a person? If you're unsure, your friendships may not be as healthy for you as you think they are.

If you suspect jealousy or hatred directed at you within your friendship circle, you're not surrounding yourself with the right people. True friends want the best for you. Your success is shared with them. They don't become bitter when you get better; they help you get better and ensure you don't become bitter!

> *Some friends want you to do well, but not too well. It's important that we do not settle for these mediocre friendships either, as they'll fill our lives with negative energy.*

We all grow and mature at different rates, but some people have slow growth because they *choose* to remain stuck. You'll often meet people who are caught up in the same routines, doing the same things with the same peers, and complaining about the same problems. These people actively resist change and don't step out of their comfort zone in search of a better life. They become comfortable with their dissatisfaction.

You may be one of these people, or they may be your close friends. You may be highly ambitious and finally pluck up the courage to go for more in your life. Your friends, on the other hand, might not get it, and the difference in frequencies between you could cause separation. For example, if you wish to grow spiritually, you may become interested in concepts that are completely alien – even scary – to your friends.

The truth is, all of your friends teach you something valuable in life. They each have a role to play. Some have temporary positions, others are permanent. It's fine to outgrow people and move on with your life. You must always focus on your own life, expanding it and growing as an individual. You can only do great things for others in the world if you genuinely feel joyful, loving and accomplished. If the people around you choose different paths or aren't quite where you are, that's okay. If they're supposed to be in your life, sooner or later they'll be there; your journeys will align again eventually.

Facing family

You can outgrow clothes, hobbies, jobs, friends – and even family members. We evolve past things that don't contribute to our joy and wellbeing.

Just because they're your family, it doesn't mean they have the best intentions for you. Many of us are taught that there's nothing more important than family. But biological relationships don't always equal supportive, close relationships. Friends can be more like family than family itself. We shouldn't conceal the fact that sometimes it's our own family members who are the most toxic people in our lives.

Ending these relationships can be the most heartbreaking because, let's face it, these people often mean the most to us, even if they do continuously put us down. It's hard to justify ending a relationship with your parents, for example, if they've done a lot for you throughout your life.

Sometimes, you don't have to. You simply need to communicate and tell them how you feel. You'll be surprised by how many people are oblivious to their toxic behaviours towards others.

When they find out that they're actually hurting you, they may very well change their ways.

We can also try to understand their intentions. Most of our loved ones do genuinely have good intentions for us. They want to see us happy, successful and prosperous. But they can be misled or limited in their view, which sometimes comes across as being negative.

A friend had an exciting idea about an online business he wanted to pursue, and looked for his parents' approval. To his dismay, their reaction wasn't quite what he'd hoped for. They ridiculed his idea and tried to talk him out of it; they simply couldn't understand how it could be profitable. Instead, they suggested that he stopped living in dreamland and focused on studying and getting the grades he needed to go to university.

He felt that his belief in his brilliant idea was dampened by their scepticism. This wasn't the first time either. He felt as though his parents were always knocking his aspirations, and as a result he perceived them as being negative towards him. He didn't want to shut his parents out of his life, because he loved them – and lived with them. But at times he felt they didn't love him!

What he failed to understand was that although his parents were critical, it wasn't entirely their fault. Their ideas about what was feasible in life and what success looked like were different from his. Their beliefs, shaped by their experiences and social conditioning, meant they had a different outlook on life.

To recognize love in spite of criticism, you have to understand that *everyone's* perspective – including your own – is limited and subjective. We all constantly gather information from everywhere, and everything we learn has an impact on what we believe and how we think – but this depends on exactly what information we've picked up.

If no one in your family has ever seen success by skipping university and starting an online business, the prospect of *you* doing this is completely new to them and may be rejected out of hand. People tend to fear what they can't understand. So make an effort to understand where your loved ones are coming from and what may be the root of their concern or cynicism.

Most people have believed the things they do for many years. You cannot expect them to drop their beliefs in an instant because of how you perceive the world. If you feel that they're being held back by their beliefs, you can offer an alternative perspective, but you can't force your beliefs on someone else.

If you want their support, you have to build their trust. This is your task, as much as it's theirs. Try to be open with them; talk to them and tell them how you feel. Involve them in your plans: give them more information or explain your alternative view; reassure them that you've thought about what will happen if you fail. You need to minimize their fear so that they have more faith. When they have more faith, they're more likely to show the positive support that you want.

My friend showed his parents an exact plan of what he wished to do, examples of success stories and even teachings by iconic figures who his family valued that supported his views. Gradually, he helped them change their outlook.

If you find yourself in a similar position, it's up to you to show your doubters that you're doing everything in your power to make your chosen path worthwhile.

If you don't prove that you're serious about what you want to do, you can't expect other people to be serious about it either.

Don't underestimate the power of leading by example. If it's the limited thinking of the people around you that makes them cold towards you, show them that they *could* break free from this unhappy state of being. Be open-minded and do your best to be warm towards them. Show them how one should behave, even if being treated unfairly. Your faith and determination may, gently and gradually, inspire a change in them. They might see how great you are as an individual and how rewarding it is to be like you!

Sometimes, simply by shifting our perspective and focusing on the positives we see in people who challenge us, we're able to feel better about our relationship with them. This is especially useful when you're living in the same house as those who dampen your spirit. This doesn't provide a full fix, but if you appreciate the good in them and create some distance until things improve, this can be a catalyst for healing.

It's vital to remember that you cannot change others unless they want to change themselves. You can influence them and facilitate change, but you cannot *make* them change. And they'll only decide to change when they have an *incentive* – such as a better life or a better relationship with you. If they don't identify a problem with their way of being, they won't be motivated to change.

In some cases, a family member's behaviour can be extreme, such as inflicting physical or emotional harm. We weren't placed on this planet to suffer at the hands – or words – of another person, regardless of our relationship with them. And pretending someone's harmful behaviour is okay is in itself harmful. If you need to cut someone off because of continued destructive behaviour, then do it with no regrets.

Being there for others

Earlier, I wrote about the importance of being around people who are in a more positive mood than you, vibrating higher, if you want to feel good. This is often a great solution, but can, naturally, have a downside for those with the higher vibration. They may find that when they're there for someone who isn't feeling great, they find it difficult to remain stable in their own emotional state. Spending time with someone who's searching for higher vibes can pull them down.

You may feel like this when a friend explains all their troubles to you and sadness suddenly spreads through your body. It's catching. I learned this lesson at university when a flatmate of mine was feeling low after being heartbroken by a girlfriend who'd ended their relationship. One night while we were out with friends, he went back to the flat early, distraught about the break-up. The girl who he was heartbroken over became extremely worried from the texts he was sending her that he'd do something to harm himself. She let us know so we could check on him.

When my friends and I got back to the flat, his door was locked and his music was turned up loud. We kept knocking on his door, but he wouldn't let us in. We started to panic and called the caretaker, who had a spare key to his room.

As we entered, we saw him curled up in bed with tears running down his face. We took a closer look at his wrists and saw the marks of what appeared to be self-inflicted cuts. In that moment, we realized that he was so low that he wanted to end his life. Fortunately, our entrance interrupted his desperation and we were able to console him.

Over the next few days, there was a very strange vibe in our flat. Everyone was shaken. The flatmate who'd attempted to take his own life didn't say much about the incident, but he did want to spend time with me. I spent my evenings with him, offering support and trying to offer gentle advice to make him feel better.

But after a while, I realized that I didn't feel like my normal self; I was starting to feel really down. I realized that as much as I wanted to be there for him, I had to think about myself, too. I felt empty, and I couldn't pour from an empty cup.

Before you try to fix someone else's vibe, make sure you're not killing your own in the process. Protect your own energy first.

I created some distance between us for a while, keeping our interactions to a minimum. Inside, I was punishing myself for not being there for him more; I felt that I had to be God-like and simply accept it. However, I was already torn apart and I knew that unless I felt good in myself, I just wouldn't be able to offer him proper support. I'd feel hypocritical for offering comfort when I was distraught myself.

He seemed to be doing okay and this gave me a little peace of mind. Eventually, I was able to get my vibration up and be there for him more effectively.

This was many years ago and since then a lot has changed. For one, I have a much greater depth of awareness and understanding. I'm fortunate to be in the position where many thousands of people feel they can share their problems with me, but because of what I've learned I can now keep my vibration steady, even if someone else's vibration is very low. There are exceptions and I'm still careful to protect my energy from people who want to drain it or abuse my willingness to help them.

If my emotional state isn't high enough to start with, I know that by trying to help someone who is feeling low, I may suffer a profound emotional impact.

If you're listening to someone ranting on about how troublesome their life is and you're not feeling great yourself, you could be heading for a major energy drain. Although lending an ear can be helpful, increasing the number of unhappy people in the world doesn't benefit anyone.

The wisest thing for you to do in this situation is to change your state by vibrating as high as you can. This is how you protect your own vibration. By doing this, you build the strength needed to help others.

Handling negative people

Not everyone is going to get you, accept you or even try to understand you. Some people will just not receive your energy well. Make peace with that and keep on moving towards your joy.

Nearly every single person in the world, no matter how kind or amazing they're perceived to be by the majority, will have at least one person who dislikes them. Only if you stayed alone in your house all day and no one saw you, spoke to you or knew of your existence, would no one show hatred towards you. You acquire haters by being a *somebody*.

I receive negative remarks from people every now and then, even if I've done a good deed. This is partly because this kind of abuse is so common online in general, particularly since people don't have to reveal their identity. Online they're free to leave bitter remarks

– things that they wouldn't dream of saying in real life – without having to take any responsibility for their words.

I remember the first time I was mocked. It was when I was five years old. I was in school and our class had to describe our parents. Everyone in my class described both their mum and dad.

When it was my turn, I described my mum and not my dad. This invited questions from other kids, who asked me what had happened to my dad. I didn't know what to say, and fortunately my teacher intervened. Truthfully, I had no idea that children were supposed to have two parents. I was used to having only my mum and I hadn't questioned it.

At breaktime, some of the kids in my class started mocking me.

They said things like, 'He hasn't even got a dad.'

'His dad is probably dead.'

'His mum is his dad.'

I became more and more wound up, and reacted with violent aggression. I got into deep trouble, despite telling the teacher why I'd done what I did.

If I hadn't been to school, I wouldn't have had that experience. Even when we're really young, it's usually a lack of understanding and compassion that creates hatred towards others. If people aren't the same as us, we're more likely to label them as misfits and to mock them. And the more people we're exposed to, the higher our chances of receiving judgement and criticism. This is because we're now in front of a large audience of individuals, each with their own perceptions of what *normal* is.

Just think about celebrities. They're only human, but because they reach so many people, they receive tremendous amounts of criticism. We talk about kindness to others but exclude celebrities as if they're not human. Sadly, everyone has their gospel but fails to practise what they preach. They're the same people reading and reciting holy words, with unholy behaviours. They're the same people who believe they're on a righteous path, but will judge others for not being on the same path as they are.

Remind yourself that negativity from others is unavoidable. With our constant exposure to the rest of the world, and our interactions with it, we're bound to face some people who have a low vibration and act unkindly towards us.

Trying to keep your distance from such people can become a huge ask when there's very little you can do to avoid them.

Here are some important reminders to help you remain peaceful when people speak negatively about you. You'll begin to realize that the best defence is silence and joy.

'Nobody can hurt me
without my permission.'

Mahatma Gandhi

Misery loves company

Unfortunately, people who are vibrating at a low frequency often want to drag others down to their level. Sometimes they'll try to expose what's wrong with you, because they can't handle everything that's right with you. They probably won't like it when others show you love or give you attention, and their resentment will probably build when, despite their efforts to make others hate you, they still love you.

The Internet is full of people who enjoy seeing other people being ridiculed and kicked while they're down. They're quick to accept negative assumptions and eager to celebrate failures. People who have made mistakes or fallen on hard times rapidly become trending topics due to a cultural addiction to the downfall of others.

People oppose progress

When you're making noise, someone will try to turn down your volume. When you're shining bright, someone will try to dim your light. It's simple: if you weren't standing out from the rest, people would have no reason to hate.

These haters are often individuals who feel threatened, jealous or hurt by our confidence as we strive for greatness. They may feel that our success will limit theirs, or fear losing their place to us. They may dislike the idea that our confidence leads us to be celebrated when they strongly desire their own praise. They may be offended by our unrestricted beliefs if theirs are constrained by a conditioned mind that feels powerless to change anything.

They want to dampen our will and drive so that their ego doesn't feel overshadowed. By belittling us, they believe they won't feel so little themselves. These people exist and they'll show up on our path to a greater life. We mustn't deny their existence, but we mustn't react either. A reaction is exactly what they want to make us feel down and protect their ego.

Hurt people hurt other people

The way people act towards the outside world illustrates what's going on in their inner world. When someone attempts to make you feel inadequate, it's because they feel inadequate themselves. Understanding this will help you handle related situations more effectively.

For example, sadness makes people act bitterly and without love; pain and internal suffering claw us into a low vibration. It causes a domino effect of hurt, because all too often people aren't in a good mood because they've been hurt by someone else who wasn't in a good mood. These newly hurt people then hurt other people, and on it goes.

But trying to heal pain by inflicting it on others doesn't work. The Indian guru and spiritual teacher Osho once likened this to banging on a wall. His view was that attacking others to relieve your pain is like someone being angry and then taking it all out on a wall, trying to cause it damage. They don't define the wall and the wall doesn't have the problem – they do. Eventually they'll end up more hurt, even though the wall has not hurt them itself.

Disliking difference

People tend to feel drawn towards individuals who resemble them in some way. This is demonstrated by a neuro-linguistic programming (NLP) technique called mirroring, which shows that mimicking an individual's behaviours encourages them to like you.

So, if you're generally loud, bubbly and full of life, and you come across someone similar, you'd probably think they're pretty cool. And if their speech patterns, body language and tone are similar to yours, you might think, 'You know what, there's something about this person I really like.' That's because they're just like you.

We can also assume the opposite to be true: people tend not to feel an affinity with individuals who are different from them. And someone different from you might think you come across as a bit strange or 'out there'. Ultimately, they won't understand you, or want to understand you, because your energy doesn't match theirs.

What goes around comes around

You've probably heard the word 'karma'. Many people are uncomfortable with this term because it's a theological concept (found in the Buddhist and Hindu religions, among others) that involves reincarnation. The belief is that your actions will have ramifications on your next life cycle; the more good deeds you do in this life, the better your next life will be.

Whether or not you believe in reincarnation, most of us accept the notion that one reaps what one sows. In science, we might recognize this as 'cause and effect', or relate it to Newton's third law – 'For every action there is an equal and opposite reaction.' And if you look through the majority of religious texts, you'll find a reference that relates to the idea that what goes around comes around.

But when people treat us unfairly, we rarely reassure ourselves that karma will catch up with them and just move on with our lives. Instead, we get caught up in our emotions while our rational mind takes a back seat.

For example, if someone is going around saying you're violent when you're clearly not, you might feel offended. If they persistently do this, you may feel anger building inside you. One day, you might get sick and tired of the accusations and react violently. Even if the rumour isn't true, your actions have now made it look as though it is.

Earlier, we learned that actions driven by a low vibrational state, such as anger, will only hurt us further, and that includes the bad karma these actions will create. So don't allow the cruelty of others to define your future.

The lonely and bored crave attention

When your life isn't interesting, you tend to focus on other people. You seek excitement and attention from hating others and provoking reactions. This is why memes are so popular on the Internet. People want others to laugh at their attempts at mocking someone else. They'll do it for likes, comments and shares – for instant gratification. This will make them feel good for a short time and as if they're doing something worthwhile. Which leads to my final point...

What people say about you says more about them than about you

When others judge you, they reveal themselves. They show their insecurities, needs, mindset, attitude, history and limitations. And they paint a clear picture of their future: they won't go very far, or live a joyful life, if they're wasting their precious time judging others.

Trying to please everyone

If you keep trying to satisfy others, you will never keep up. In the end, you will satisfy neither them nor yourself.

Hopefully, it's clear to you now that we do a lot of things in order to be accepted, but if we want to do well in life and maintain our peace, we have to be a little selfish. We'll never be able to satisfy absolutely everyone, and that's exactly why we shouldn't even try. Give up the habit of being a people-pleaser and start pleasing *you*!

As someone who likes helping others with their personal problems, I've found it difficult to stop trying to make everyone happy. In the past, I'd receive hundreds of emails a week from people telling me their problems and asking for help. Naturally, I'd want to assist them.

Some people write very lengthy emails, upwards of 2,000 words. I don't believe in doing things half-heartedly, so my response would always be thorough. By the time I'd read and replied to an email this long, I'd have used up a great deal of time.

Responding to everyone was virtually impossible and some people became irate because they felt I was ignoring them. It made me feel terrible and I began to punish myself for it. Although I had other more pressing tasks to complete, I devoted an unreasonable amount of time to replying to these emails.

I became overwhelmed. I realized I couldn't please everyone, so I shouldn't attempt to, nor should I be too hard on myself. It was important to prioritize my needs and this is exactly what I did. I've never looked back.

I'm sure you can relate in some way to my experience of being raised in a very judgemental community. As a child, certain career choices were sold to me as reflecting well within the community. If I became a doctor, I'd be considered intelligent, rich and philanthropic.

Yet my community would still judge me if I became a doctor. For example, if I remained single until I was 30 years old because I was working all the time, then it would indicate something was wrong with me. If I didn't have my own house, I'd be deemed to be experiencing financial hardship. If I became a doctor and had everything apart from a child, they'd assume I was having fertility problems. That's how these communities work. Someone will always see a flaw in you.

Sometimes, I'm accused of being arrogant or stubborn for not giving much thought to the opinions of others. It's an extension of a judgemental ethos that leads people to this conclusion.

Constructive opinions can be very beneficial to our growth, but destructive ones that demoralize us don't have a positive purpose. Abuse and criticism disguised as 'feedback' doesn't deserve your attention.

Let your good vibes protect you

Some negative people are allergic to positivity. Be so positive that they can't stand being near you.

After I committed myself to living life in a more optimistic manner, I gave up my unhealthy habits and embraced positivity as often as I could. I then began noticing that some of the people I associated with didn't like this. They preferred my old behaviour – they wanted me to complain and to be aggressive and judgemental.

It was as if my attitude was too positive for them. Some people labelled me as fake. I could understand why: I'd gone from someone who complained a lot to someone who made a conscious effort to see the good in things. I'd taken myself to a different frequency from them, emotionally. The further you are emotionally from another person, the less real you appear to them. This is based on the Law of Vibration. This distance can make both individuals feel uncomfortable around one another because you just don't vibe together. Sometimes this is a great indicator of whom you need to keep your distance from.

What was apparent from my new, positive behaviour was that it was pushing certain people away. When people were rude to me, I started reacting kindly to them. I didn't show up to the battle they were preparing for. This repelled them because they didn't have an answer for my response to their rudeness. This was great, because those people were the ones on a much lower frequency than I was, but who had no interest in raising theirs; they were too comfortable in their cynical ways. Our energies were incompatible and they shrank from my field of existence. I didn't need to distance myself from them because they'd done the job for me.

Dare to leave a toxic job

Believe it or not, your purpose is not to be in a job you dislike for the rest of your life.

If you knew of a certain alley notorious as a murder site, you'd choose to avoid it. You'd know that by walking through it, you'd risk something terrible happening to you, regardless of your state of mind.

Less dramatically, if you're invited to a birthday celebration where you know someone who regularly verbally attacks you will be present, you could choose to avoid it and protect your inner peace. You know your attendance will only attract drama.

But there are similarly toxic settings that are much harder to avoid. One of the most common is your place of work. There might be people there who make your life a misery, but you can't just stay at home.

I experienced this with a new manager at the office job I mentioned earlier. When I look back at the experience, I don't entirely blame him for his actions. He had his own life and his own pressures from those who he reported to. And I wasn't the best employee because I didn't enjoy the work I was doing so I wasn't engaged in it.

Although I was thankful for having a decent job, all the signs suggested that I needed to leave and pursue my passions. I knew I wanted to spread positivity in the world and help people to better their lives. So one day I took a massive, courageous step: I quit my job and jumped into the unknown.

It was a huge risk. I left with very little financial security, as I didn't have much money saved. Some might say I was bold and brave; others might put it down to naivety. But after I left I woke up each day with a rush of gratitude. Even though I had a few financial burdens, there was no price I could put on the sense of peace I'd found. I was soon able to follow my passions and start a lifestyle blog, sharing personal development articles.

I've never regretted my decision and I'm thankful for all the difficulties I faced before I started over; for example, the wounds from working the wrong jobs gave me wisdom and resolve that's helped me create a better life for myself and others. Nonetheless, it's very common for people to become stuck in harmful workplaces. But they push us into unhealthy mental states and greatly affect our wellbeing.

Leaving an unfulfilling job is daunting, and most of the time financial obligations prevent you from saying 'enough is enough' and acting on it. We all crave security and comfort, and entering the unknown can be scary. But you can't be certain of security from a job, either; you have no control over your salary, pay rises, promotions or anything else about your job – even that you'll continue to have it.

When you recognize that you deserve better than the toxic situation you're trapped in, be daring enough to move on. You don't have to rush the process, but the longer you stay in harmful conditions, the more you sabotage your own life.

PART FOUR

Accepting Yourself

Introduction

You won't be important to other people all the time, and that's why you have to be important to yourself. Learn to enjoy your own company. Take care of yourself. Encourage positive self-talk – and become your own support system. Your needs matter, so start meeting them yourself. Don't rely on others.

Someone once posed the question: 'If I asked you to name all the things you love, how long would it take for you to name yourself?'

This question serves as a reminder that many of us neglect self-love. It's the result of a common problem within our society: we're conditioned to care more about what others think of us than what we think of ourselves.

Learning to interact effectively with other people and getting them to like you will help you to achieve your goals. But there's a deeper issue that must be addressed first: *Do you like yourself?*

We learn to care about how others feel about us but avoid focusing on how we feel about ourselves. This creates a society in which people try to impress others in order to be liked, but deep down they remain unsatisfied because they don't like themselves.

Admittedly, it's nice when your talents are recognized, when your work is rewarded, your achievements applauded or your looks appreciated. In these moments we justify our existence. We're flattered. We feel loved. We feel important. Life feels good.

But we continue on a perpetual mission to please others, to prove our worth. We create our own financial pressures by buying things we don't need, just so we can impress people who care little for our wellbeing. We change ourselves to fit in, rather than changing the world by being ourselves. We alter our natural beauty to adapt to societal expectations. We strive for endless external goals while neglecting our own spiritual growth.

The power of love and kindness is enormous, and sharing it with others can transform the world. But we must also be kind and loving towards ourselves. Instead of trying to change who you are, start giving yourself permission to feel good. Transform your own world and you'll hone the skills needed to change the world around you.

If, as happens very often, we don't treat ourselves with the kindness and respect we deserve, we become insecure, and this affects our confidence, attitude and health. This results in a struggle to show love towards others in the way we want to, which, in turn, affects the expressions of love we *receive*. People tend to enjoy being around, and fall in love with, those who gracefully accept themselves. For this reason, self-love is a vital element in building strong relationships.

Let's say a young woman called Kierah lacks self-love and show signs of insecurity in her relationship with her partner, Troy, because she doesn't feel she's as pretty as the other girls Troy knows. This makes her behave in ways that, from Troy's perspective, display a lack of respect and trust, such as going through his phone and reading his private messages. Regardless of whether they genuinely love each other, their relationship suffers because Kierah lacks self-love. Kierah's behaviour begins to affect Troy's wellbeing. He then starts to believe that her actions indicate that she doesn't truly love him, and as a result his own self-esteem is damaged. Their relationship enters a downward spiral and eventually comes to an end.

When you accept yourself as you are, you put emphasis on your own wellbeing and joy – and you'll be content with the idea that not everyone will accept you as you are. You'll know your worth, so you won't care if others don't recognize it. In fact, you'll come to understand *why* they don't recognize it: unfortunately, because most people don't accept themselves, they search for flaws in others.

We're back where we started: the importance of loving yourself unconditionally.

The ideas that follow in Chapter 1 will enhance your awareness and understanding of exactly why you hold your current beliefs, so you can make meaningful changes to your life. This journey of personal growth will guide you towards self-acceptance and bring joyful experiences into your world.

Appreciate your physical beauty

It's great to take care of yourself when it comes to physical appearance. We should always feel comfortable in our own skin and looking after your body is a healthy habit. The fact that you have a body at all is incredible. You're a reflection of the wonder of nature.

Whether you believe in God or not, when the world was created it wasn't given rules or instructions to help humankind assess what physical beauty is. No – these ideas were formed by us and are today often moderated and manipulated by the mainstream media.

You can only recognize your own beauty if you practise self-love, but I'll be honest with you: it's difficult. With media platforms playing on our insecurities, it's hard not to compare ourselves with others.

We're bombarded by images showing people with conventionally attractive bodies. We know that most of these images aren't real, that they've been edited or doctored in order to sell an idea, a product or a dream, but we easily forget this and they quickly magnify confidence issues.

We define our physical flaws in relation to what we're told is the 'perfect body'. We're constantly told what beauty looks like and if we don't question this, these endless messages implant in our heads a subconscious definition of what it means to be beautiful. Anything that doesn't match the popular definition of beauty appears to us as a flaw and makes us judgemental, always assessing physical beauty against that benchmark. This not only affects how we perceive others, but also how we perceive ourselves.

Through my work I've been fortunate enough to engage with many young people. Some have a large online following, while others are just typical teenagers. I got to know one of the well-known figures really well, and was sad to learn that she had acquired a lot of hatred as a result of a sharp increase in popularity. When she posted natural shots of herself on social media, she came under fire for being ugly. The pressure of being judged and ridiculed led her to have cosmetic surgery to maintain her public image.

Don't let socially constructed ideas about beauty lower your self-esteem. There are no rules to beauty. Accept and love yourself as you are. Embrace your flaws and get comfortable in your own skin. Wear your imperfections like they don't need a season to be fashionable.

But the hate continued. First, she was judged for not appearing perfect by society's standards, and then she was judged for trying to fix it. The truth is clear: you simply cannot satisfy everyone.

I also spoke to a young woman who admired this public figure, and she admitted that she often felt insecure due to comparing her physical appearance with her idol's. She admitted that this even made her act in unloving ways towards other people – she thought nothing of leaving negative remarks about how other public figures looked, just because they weren't as beautiful as her idol. I pointed out that similar comments were the reason her idol had resorted to surgery.

There's a culture of negativity swirling around the Internet and even rebounding on those we claim to like. Constant comparison of one human against another drives you into a web of negative and loveless thoughts.

Never allow society's ideals for physical beauty to devalue your existence. Nearly all those ideals are driven from insecurity and a desire to feel more confident – or to sell something. If you think about it, how many businesses would go out of business if you truly accepted yourself?

The size of your jeans doesn't define you.
The colour and shade of your skin doesn't define you.
That number on the scales doesn't define you.
Those marks on your face don't define you.
Those expectations don't define you.
Those opinions don't define you.

Your personal beauty isn't for everyone, and that's fine. It doesn't mean you're less beautiful than any other human being. Perfection is subjective and based entirely on perception. Wear your 'imperfections' proudly, because they make you unique. Never stop appreciating your own beauty.

If you feel you'd rather be someone other than yourself, you're not alone. But if you can recognize and embrace your own unique beauty, you can live with authenticity and be proud of who you are. A person who accepts themself as they are can inspire the world. And that can be you. You could show the world how to reach joy through self-acceptance.

Compare only with yourself

Ignore what everyone else is doing. Your life is not about everyone else; it's about you. Instead of focusing on their path, pay attention to your own. That's where your journey is taking place.

Comparison is one of the most common reasons why we experience sadness. I admit that comparison has stolen my joy on many occasions. It got to the stage where I was often embarrassed by my life because it wasn't as attractive as the lives of those around me. I remember during school I'd rarely invite my friends to my house because I felt embarrassed by its size and condition.

It's very difficult in this world not to compare yourself with others. During one of my meditations, I came across a memory of a wedding I attended as a child. I joined in some games with the other kids; I must have only been 10 years old. There was a boy who was a few years older than me and he was dictating what game we'd play next. He appeared to be the leader.

There was one instance where we'd all stopped playing and this leader took a good look around at us all to see what we were wearing. He was dressed very smartly in expensive designer-branded clothes.

He was very rude to the other kids about their clothes. I started getting a little anxious as he was coming round to me. My clothes were far from expensive. I didn't want him to mock me in front of the others and call me poor. This would've made me feel embarrassed, particularly as I was already insecure about my home life.

Fortunately for me, there was a distraction and I got away without being called out. However, the fear of being judged for my apparent lack of wealth never left me. It just got worse as I got older. On special days at school when we got to wear what we wanted, kids who didn't wear branded clothes were often picked on.

I'm not sure how my mum did it, with three of us kids and a minimum-wage job, but she ensured we weren't ever in this position. Nevertheless, if I was wearing Nike-branded shoes, they'd be the cheapest ones you could buy. I'd keep looking at the kids who were wearing the expensive ones, feeling poor and insignificant. I wanted what they had and these moments reminded me of everything I lacked.

Children can acquire the habit of comparing themselves to others from their parents. Parents want the best for their child, so they might celebrate other kids as a way to motivate their own child to do better. For example, they might say, 'Saira got straight As in her exams. She's so bright and has an amazing future ahead of her.'

As harmless as the intention might be, this has the potential to undermine a child's abilities, especially if they're not being praised for their achievements, too. If direct comparisons are drawn, then a child can feel degraded and worthless. Lines such as, 'You should be as smart as Saira,' are extremely damaging and can leave a child forever feeling that they're not good enough.

Brand marketing encourages us to draw comparisons all the time. You're not trendy if it's not Apple, you're not successful if it's not Lamborghini and you're not fashionable if it's not something an A-list celebrity wore. These implications are made through cunning marketing strategies devised to prey on fear and low self-esteem.

When we compare, we always look at those who we perceive to be doing better than us; rarely do we look at those who are facing bigger struggles than us. So we never feel grateful for what we *do* have.

Looking to others for inspiration is fine, but there's a difference between inspiration and envy.

The rise of social media is proving problematic, too. Younger age groups of children and adults are now becoming heavily absorbed in it, unaware that social media presents rose-tinted versions of life as the truth, and it's against this fiction that they're comparing themselves.

I've learned that sometimes real couples who are on the brink of giving up on their relationship will post a multitude of loving images online so that no one realizes what they're going through and judges them. (Not that these couples would be likely to share their arguments and disagreements online instead; no one says halfway through an argument, 'Hold on, let me take a picture of this.') People will post remarks saluting how amazing the couple's relationship is and how they wish they could have the same thing –

drawing a comparison. They have no idea what's happening behind the scenes. We cannot see or understand everything from one shot.

Comparing our lives with others' that we see online is a waste of energy. People only share photos in which they look attractive, happy and successful; not when they're tired, scared and lonely.

Similarly, I've also learned that some on-screen relationships are manufactured for the purpose of benefiting those involved – for example, to build up their public profiles. That's why some of these couples appear to have more love towards the camera than towards each other. Despite this, their snapshots can still be sold.

Remember, if someone is sharing images or videos of their wonderful life, you don't know what they went through to get it. For every triumph, there might have been a bucket load of blood, sweat and tears. Even for some of the public figures who are constantly seen online as being in love, there might be a history of rejection and bullying. For every gorgeous photo, there may be 50 that were deleted.

I've come across people who are completely different on social media from who they are in real life. The truth is distorted with filters and inspirational captions to make everything seem better than it is. We all know this, but it's easy to forget.

It appeals to human nature to turn to social media for instant validation through likes, comments and followers. When we engage with social media, our brain releases dopamine, a hormone that makes us feel good (and is also involved in addiction). Have you considered that you might be comparing your life with those of people who use social media to fill a void in themselves because they've forgotten how to practise self-love?

This isn't about what other people are doing or sharing online. It's not about what they're up to in life or how far they've gone. It's about you. Your competition is you. Outdoing yourself is your daily task, and that's where your comparison should be directed: on the person you were yesterday. If you want to be the greatest version of yourself, you have to keep the focus on your own life and goals.

Competing with others encourages bitterness, not betterment.

No two single journeys are the same. You're on your own path. We all move through life at our own pace and reach different stages at different times. Someone else might already be at the most interesting part of their show while you're still making preparations behind the scenes for yours. This doesn't mean that you won't get your opportunity to get on stage and shine.

Look at other people's lives and applaud their successes. And then continue to pursue your own. Be grateful for what you have right now. And remember how far you've come as you continue in the direction of your dreams.

Value your inner beauty

How many times have you heard someone being called beautiful for their mind or for their actions towards others? It's pretty rare, especially in relation to the number of times people are called beautiful for their physical appearance. People too often label others 'beautiful' for superficial reasons while overlooking those who demonstrate inner beauty: unconditional love and kindness. This is because these qualities are, sadly, not interesting to people who pursue superficial successes.

For this reason, it's very common for people to change the way they appear in order to reflect the ideals of beauty that society has been conditioned to worship – but it's far less common to change the way you think and act.

If we strive to call more people beautiful because of their kindness, then we'll become more interested in changing the way we behave. Beauty is so much more than physical appearance.

Experiencing physical attraction towards someone doesn't mean you should invest your energy in them. Their heart, mind and spirit must be beautiful to you, too. A luxury sports car is useless without an engine, as is someone who is beautiful to you only physically; it will be difficult to move forward in life with them if they don't share your inner values.

Physical beauty does nothing but satisfy physical needs. Only those with real substance can satisfy the hearts, minds and souls of others.

Real beauty must be deeper than what meets the eye. It must go beyond the skin. Our bodies can always change but our internal beauty can last a lifetime. This is where your value is and why it's so important to spend time on building your character. After all, you can buy surgery but you cannot purchase a new personality. You can attract many people with your looks, but you can only hold on to a great person with what you have on the inside.

Celebrate your achievements

We assume success is about being famous, rich and owning expensive things. But if you've pulled yourself out of a dark place, that's a great success in itself. Don't forget that you're winning each day you don't give up and you make it through to the next.

Did you know that you're achieving great things every day? It probably doesn't seem like it if you're always looking ahead to the next thing. Nevertheless, many of the things you've achieved today are things you dreamed about in the past. You just don't notice them in the moment they happen. Or they pass you by too quickly.

Although we shouldn't get so comfortable with our achievements that we become complacent and stop moving forwards, we should make time to celebrate them. Otherwise you'll look back on your life and think you didn't do anything significant. But if this were true, your life would always have remained the same.

We're too hard on ourselves. We remember everything that we've done wrong, but hardly ever think about the things we've done right. Does that sound familiar? If it does, it's because you're too self-critical.

You have to give yourself a pat on the back every now and then. You've done things some people said you couldn't do. You've done things even *you* thought you couldn't do. Be proud of yourself. You've fought hard to get where you are today. Acknowledging this will bring contentment and raise your vibration.

Respect your uniqueness

Your individuality is a blessing, not a burden. If you try to be like everyone else, your life will be no greater than theirs. By following the crowd, you'll become a part of it and fail to stand out. By travelling the same road as them, you won't get the chance to see anything different from what they see.

As young children, we're regularly reminded that we're all individuals and should have no shame in being ourselves. We're encouraged to pursue our wildest dreams! But as we get older, our world of possibility shrinks. People say, 'Yes, be yourself... but not like that!' or 'You can be anything in the world... but *this* is the right path to take.'

In psychology, the concept of 'social proof' suggests that people like to follow the crowd. If everyone else is doing it, you assume it's the right thing to do. Other people influence your actions more than you realize. For example, if you had to pick between two new bars and you could see that one was packed while the other isn't, you'd assume that the empty one sucked and the popular one was much better! But just because everyone else is doing it does *not* mean it's right. Slavery used to be legal, but now nearly everyone would agree that it's inhumane, degrading and immoral.

Start to question your actions. Why do you do what you do, and choose what you choose? Are you doing what you really think is right, or are you following the crowd? If you discover your choices are frequently dictated by the views of others, you know you're relinquishing control over your life. Without control, we panic and end up in low vibrational states, such as anxiety. Ultimately, we end up having no control over how much joy we experience, as we become slaves to other people's opinions.

Fear and scarcity are commonly used to control society. I've known many people who, instead of living the life they'd have chosen, have lived the life they were told to by others in the form of well-meaning guidance and support. And while some people *want* what's best for you, they may not *understand* what's best for you. They may also make decisions for you based on fear that's been passed on to them by someone else.

You can listen to the crowd
or you can listen to your soul
and be on your own stage.

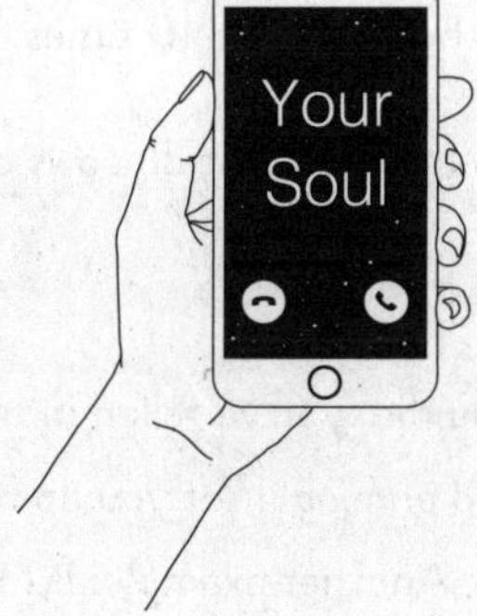

But you shouldn't feel like you're living someone else's beliefs. You shouldn't feel like you have to meet everyone else's expectations or live your life a certain way to gain their approval. You shouldn't feel like you have to shy away from being who you really are, from your uniqueness. Life shouldn't feel limiting.

The truth is that, either way, you're going to be judged, whether you live life on your own terms or on other people's.

Someone once said that a tiger doesn't lose sleep over the opinion of sheep. The tiger isn't swayed by judgements from animals whose behaviour is dictated by social conditioning. The sheep constantly seeks validation, changes direction and loses its own identity; therefore, it remains lost and ill fated.

Say the word 'silk' 10 times out loud.

Now tell me: what do cows drink?

Did you say 'milk'?

If you did, you've fallen into the trap of a psychological technique called *priming*. I set you up for a particular answer, even though it's false. Another example: if I told you a story about how I was lost in the middle of nowhere once and had no idea how to get out, and then told you to complete the word 'st_ck', you'd be more likely to say 'stuck' instead of 'stick'.

Priming also provides cues to help the memory without realizing the connection. Imagine if you could set people up to think and act in a certain way, without knowing. This is exactly what marketing companies do all the time to increase sales.

Authenticity is rare these days, and many of our actions are at the suggestion of someone else. Without drawing you into paranoia, we're easily reprogrammed to satisfy the needs of another human being – or, indeed, of a corporation.

Don't let your individuality get taken away from you, just so you can fit in with the rest of society. Embrace your uniqueness. Are you considered weird? Awesome! This is only because most people are living inside an imaginary box and you don't fit in it; and we're led to believe that when you don't fit society's needs, something is wrong with you. Who wants to be bounded by a box that isn't even there? Not me! Freedom has no constraints.

We can always improve ourselves and grow as individuals. We can step out of our comfort zone and challenge ourselves. But society often makes us feel like we're wrong for just being ourselves.

They will call you quiet because you're
perfectly happy in silence.

They will call you weak because you
avoid conflict and drama.

They will call you obsessed for being
passionate about the things you love.

They will call you rude for not
engaging in social pleasantries.

They will call you arrogant for having self-respect.

They will call you boring for not being extrovert.

They will call you wrong for having different beliefs.

They will call you shy when you choose
not to interact in small talk.

They will call you weird because you choose
not to conform to societal trends.

They will call you fake for trying
your best to remain positive.

They will call you a loner because you're
comfortable being on your own.

They will call you lost for not following
the same route as others.

They will call you a geek for being
a knowledge-seeker.

They will call you ugly for not
looking like celebrities.

They will call you dumb for not being an academic.

They will call you crazy for thinking
differently from others.

They will call you cheap for
knowing value for money.

They will call you disloyal for distancing
yourself from negative people.

Let them call you what they want. You don't have to play the part they want you to play. Create your own part to play in the world.

Be kind and forgive yourself

Forgive yourself for the bad decisions you've made, for the times you lacked belief, for the times you hurt others and yourself. Forgive yourself for all the mistakes you've made. What matters most is that you're willing to move forward with a better mindset.

How often do you find yourself disrespecting your own intelligence when you make a mistake? Do you ever ask yourself discouraging questions like, 'Why can't I do this?' 'Why am I so ugly?' or 'Why do I keep failing?'

That inner voice we have can be very critical. This type of question is often a presupposition, forcing you to accept the ideas in the questions as truth. It's a highly effective way to put yourself down.

But you must make sure the voice in your head is always kind to you. You'll encounter many people in life who are willing to put you down, but *you* shouldn't be one of them. You cannot expect others to be kind to you if you're not kind to yourself. You have to change your internal dialogue so it supports you in life. Instead of telling yourself that you're dumb for making a mistake, tell yourself that you're only human and you'll do better next time.

Your words are creative energy – an idea we'll expand on in the next section. They're extremely powerful in either supporting you or limiting your life experience. When you use words to belittle yourself, you diminish your own joy.

Do you still punish yourself for the mistakes you made as a child? More often than not the answer is no, because we realize that we were young and naive, and most of us have learned from them. They've allowed us to become better. This self-forgiveness should apply to your recent mistakes, too.

Every mistake you make can help you to improve as a person. But to make use of the lesson within each of your mistakes, you must first learn to let them go. Accept what has happened. Breathe it in, breathe it out and let it go. You're only human and you're allowed to continue with life, regardless of the magnitude of the mistake. Don't punish yourself for what you've done, and instead focus on what you can do better.

Beating yourself up will not change the situation.
It's what you strive for next that matters most.

Have you ever met someone you haven't seen for a long time, and they tell you, 'You've grown up so much!'? And if they'd talked to someone else about you before you'd met again, they'd probably have talked about the version of you who they last knew; someone from the past?

The truth is that 'You in the Past' was probably completely different from who you are now. So if someone judges you for your past, it's their problem. They're the ones who are living in a place that no longer exists. If they don't understand that people grow up and mature, they probably have some growing of their own to do. Don't let anyone use your past as an excuse to judge you; they're only trying to restrict you from building a blissful future. Remember that nothing stays the same, including you, and think back to all of your achievements and accomplishments.

It's just as important that you let go of the past, too. People may have done things to you in the past that you feel are unforgivable. You might not even remember what they did, but you hang on to how they made you feel. Attaching yourself to these ill feelings will only be destructive to your mood, dragging your vibration down.

When you forgive people you don't improve the past, you improve your present and future. You give yourself more peace and build more positive energy internally.

Those who cannot forgive people who've hurt them will only fall victim to them. Imagine having a major fall out with someone because they betrayed you. Initially, you're livid and hurt. You cut yourself loose from them and eventually you forget about it – until you see them again. At this point you replay memories of what they did to you and your pain returns, because you haven't actually forgiven them. This will dampen your spirits and could lead you to make destructive decisions.

Forgiveness isn't about condoning someone's poor behaviour and it doesn't always mean that you need to invite individuals back into your life; it simply means that you'll no longer allow them power over your thoughts and control over your emotional state. That way, they cannot dictate your destiny.

PART FIVE

Manifesting Goals: Mind Work

Introduction

'Whatever the mind of man can conceive and believe, it can achieve.'

Napoleon Hill

When trying to manifest your goals, it's important to keep a high vibration. Feelings are returned on a like-for-like basis, so it's crucial for you to master everything you've learned in the previous sections of this book.

However, without doubt, your beliefs are fundamental when it comes to manifestation. If you don't believe in something, you'll rarely see it in your life. So let's spend some time exploring the importance of our beliefs and how they affect our reality.

The importance of positive thinking

Positive thinking is the act of choosing ideas that empower you over those that limit you.

I'm certain that a positive mind gives you a positive life. Let's just analyse that statement from a purely logical angle, without any mystic correlations. If you view something as negative, how can it also be positive at the same time? Therefore, how can one ever evaluate life as being positive, from a negative sense of perception?

A positive mind is greater than a negative mind. Positive thinking is the act of choosing thoughts and actions that support us rather than hinder us, and it brings the best outcome in any situation.

For example, a cricket batsman needs six runs to win a game from the last ball. If he's fearful and believes he can't hit a six to win the game, he probably won't attempt it, so he won't manage it.

However, if he picks an empowering thought such as *I can hit this six*, he'll try, and have a chance of succeeding. Either way, the batsman can be bowled out – but the mindset is different. The empowering thought creates a possibility, while the limiting thought eradicates his chances.

A negative thought such as *You can't do it*, will discourage you from taking steps towards achieving a goal. Obviously, you're then less likely to achieve the goal.

A positive thought such as *You can do it*, will allow you to try – giving you a greater chance of achieving your goal.

One thought restricts you, while the other moves you closer to what you want.

Believing that something is impossible means you're too focused on the barriers to success. I remember a child telling me that he couldn't play top-level football and therefore wanted to give up on his dream. He had no reason to believe in it because he looked at his life and saw the task as unrealistic; it seemed impossible from where he stood.

His friend was at a similar skill level but had a completely opposite attitude. When I asked the more optimistic youngster why he believed he could reach top level, he told me about other footballers and their success stories. He saw the task as realistic because his focus was on possibility, not impossibility.

I do this all the time to give myself hope and to change my perspective. When I had no home, a lot of the things I've since achieved might have seemed unrealistic. But I was inspired by people who'd had tough starts in life yet gone on to achieve incredible things. I said to myself, 'If they can do it, why can't I?' I ended up changing my focus to what *could* be done, rather than what *couldn't* be done. Every great accomplishment in the world has grown from the idea that it's possible.

Every single one of your thoughts is either helping you move forward in life or holding you back. Positive thinking is about favouring the one that moves you forward. And it's never too late to change your thoughts and reshape your beliefs to support, rather than hinder, yourself.

You can't move forward with thoughts that hold you back.

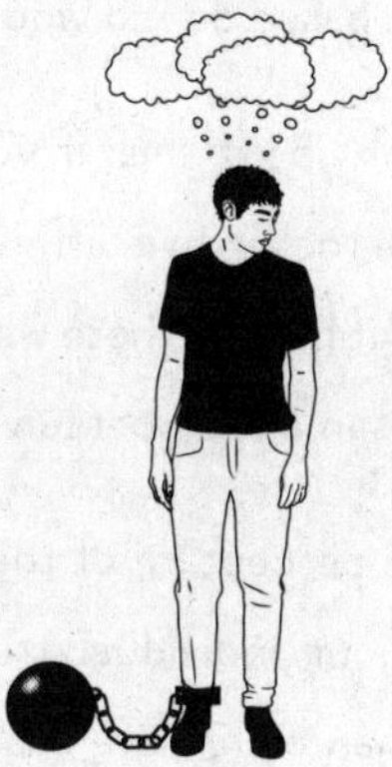

Your mentality is your reality

'Whether you think you can or think you can't, you are right.'

Henry Ford

The philosopher Immanuel Kant pointed out over 200 years ago that all our experiences, including all the colours, sensations and objects we perceive, are just representations in our mind. Reality is only based on individual perception.

Think about this: if you asked 100 different people to describe a large rock in five different ways, someone hearing those descriptions might believe there were 500 different rocks. Of course, it's in fact the same rock perceived in 500 different ways.

Our perception of the world is rooted in our beliefs. These beliefs are our individual truths that build our subjective realities. All human beings are basically just belief systems. A belief is a feeling of certainty about a particular thing; it's a passive knowing. We live our lives based on the beliefs that we've acquired through our experiences and accumulation of knowledge. Consequently, we all view the world differently.

It's useful for our personal growth to be open to the beliefs of others, and to be willing to change our beliefs if we're convinced that an alternative way of looking at something provides a more accurate and empowering view. But we shouldn't change our beliefs just because of others. Instead, we should question our own beliefs and ask ourselves, 'Do my beliefs help me live a life I truly love?' and 'How many of my beliefs are my own – and how many were given to me?'

Your mentality forms your reality. So the next time someone tells you you're being unrealistic about your goal and to come back to reality, realize that it's only their reality that they're talking about, not yours.

Believing in something is the key to seeing it. If you don't believe in it, it's not true to you so it can't be your reality.

As we know from the Law of Vibration, when we believe in negative things, we experience negative things. These negative experiences continue to reinforce the initial beliefs, making you an even bigger believer in them. And an unhappy truth can become even truer unless you decide to change your beliefs.

Understanding the subconscious mind

It is your subconscious mind that is responsible for your beliefs. All that you perceive is a result of what you accept as true in your subconscious mind.

The conscious mind thinks, the subconscious mind absorbs. Your conscious mind is your garden and your subconscious mind is like deep, fertile soil. Seeds of both success and failure can be planted in this soil without any discernment. Your conscious mind plays the role of the gardener, choosing which seeds are sown in your soil.

But most of us allow both good and bad seeds to fall within this soil. This means that limiting ideas are among those constantly taking root in our subconscious, since they're repeatedly sown there. As the subconscious doesn't evaluate these ideas, they gradually reshape our beliefs. This means fearful, jealous and power-hungry individuals will constantly feed bad seeds into your mind that will limit your potential in life. You might be told to 'Wake up' and 'Be realistic'.

Deeply habitual thinking that stems from undesirable subconscious impressions will lead you away from your true goals in life, but the truth is, once you mute the noise of the world, you'll realize there's nothing you can't do.

Going beyond thoughts

If you can't change a situation, change your perception of it. That's where your personal power is. Either be controlled – or be in control.

Growing up, I lived in a somewhat racist neighbourhood. Put it this way: if I wanted to play outside, as kids did back then, I'd spend the first half-hour fighting at least two or three kids. Eventually, I'd be drawn to fight their older brothers, too.

When they told me to go back to my own country, I was offended. This was my country and it was my right to be able to play outside. I remember thinking that no one should have the right to belittle me because of the colour of my skin. This thought built up so much rage inside me that, although I didn't like fighting, I felt – ironically – that fighting was the only way I could defend my freedom and create peace. Every time someone was racist towards me, my automatic response was violence. My violence was born from anger, which is a defence against pain. Yet I wasn't a violent person; I'd often physically hurt kids and then right away I'd feel guilty and ask them if they were okay.

But the notion of violence creating peace is a misconception we commonly observe on the news today. When I won a fight, it only encouraged more people to get involved. Soon enough, I stopped playing outside because the drama wasn't worth it.

Our brains are clever. They want to make life easy for us and to do as little thinking as possible. (This might sound a little strange, especially if you're a chronic overthinker.) So the brain is optimized to make subconscious decisions based on previous emotions attached to experiences. This autopilot behaviour created by repetition allows us to move through our day without having to relearn processes, such as driving, and without having to think through all the minutiae of daily life.

However, since our subconscious mind has no awareness, it can unwittingly hold us captive to unhealthy behaviour. The fact that I felt bad every time I reacted violently to the abuse I was subjected to made me realize that *I* wasn't my reactions; I was conditioned to react like that by my past experiences, and I didn't question my reaction because I lacked awareness.

You are not your thoughts. You are the witness of each thought.

By this principle, I never actually thought, 'I am angry'; I was simply *aware* of this thought and emotion. By cultivating this awareness, we can learn to make better decisions as to how to act.

How we perceive an event determines how we experience it. Events are neutral, but we give them labels. When a *bad* event happens, take a pause – and then observe your thoughts. This is making the unconscious mind conscious; replacing thought with awareness. Only once you notice your thoughts can you make a choice as to how you respond. Meditation is a powerful tool for honing this skill.

Look at any disempowering thought as not really *you* and let it pass by. Or select a more empowering thought. For example, if you've just lost your job, you could focus on the thought that says you're going to be unemployed and broke, which will make you feel hopeless and lower your vibration. Or you could focus on the opportunity to find a new job that pays more. The second thought will make you feel better and raise your vibration.

This is the practice of living consciously: unlearning and reconditioning the mind so you can have more freedom to be who you really are. It's not a quick process, but with dedication it will allow you to shift from a cycle of negative thinking to a new mode of positive thinking.

In short: rather than trying to control external events, concentrate on controlling how your mind responds to them. This gives you back your personal power and is the key to a happy life.

Your goal isn't to get rid of negative thoughts; it's to change your response to them.

One thought is all it takes

You're only ever one positive thought away from a more desirable outcome.

Chaos theory is a field of study in mathematics, with applications over disciplines including physics, biology, economics and philosophy. It suggests that even a tiny difference in initial parameters can lead to complex and unpredictable results. This is often known as the butterfly effect: the flapping of a butterfly's wings in the Amazon could cause tiny atmospheric changes that, over a certain time period, could affect weather patterns as far away as New York.

For example, imagine we repeatedly fired a cannon ball from a particular position and angle, with the exact same conditions each time. Using mathematics and physics, we could calculate where the ball will land each time. It's predictable. However, if you change anything in the slightest way – such as the position, angle or air resistance – the ball will land in a different place.

Similarly, if we change just one thought to a more positive one, and we really believe in it, we change our whole perception of the world. This new perception has the power to change outcomes.

We cannot rely on our environment to create new outcomes; it's not usually within our control. However, as the cannon barrel in your life, you can easily fire a ball at a different angle or from a different height, so that it lands further away or in a different place, simply by changing your thoughts. This *is* within your control.

Changing your beliefs

It would be nice to change your beliefs overnight, but this is an astoundingly difficult thing to achieve. As we've established, our beliefs are dug deep into the soils of our subconscious mind. When we accept notions without question, we live with them for most of our lives. Some of these ideas make sense to us, but don't empower us. They limit our potential in life.

The first step is to identify which core beliefs you want to change. For example, one of my core beliefs was: 'I can't change my future, so I'll never be able to achieve big things.'

These beliefs didn't make me feel good, but if I'd tried to change them right away, I'd have felt as though I were lying to myself. After all, these beliefs were my truth. But why did I think they were *the* truth?

When I confronted my restricting beliefs, I discovered that I believed what I did because of what I'd been told by someone I looked up to. They'd told me that everyone is given a specific life and we have no control over it whatsoever. Apparently, some people were just born lucky and others weren't, and we have to accept it. We shouldn't waste our time trying to create something different. It was explained much more subtly than I've described it. However, not only was this ideology fed into my mind from a young age, but it was also reiterated by everyone around me. And so I believed that I had no power to change the course of my life.

As I got older and things got harder, my own beliefs saddened me. I felt I had no alternative and I must live like this because that's what was intended for me. But I didn't want to believe this – I wanted a way out.

I started to question the validity of my beliefs. I also became sceptical about how credible the source of these beliefs was. Sure, they came from someone who was respected and everyone around me confirmed them, but none of these people were the type of person I aspired to.

In my late teens, I wanted to be rich and famous, so I decided to study people who *were* rich and famous, and see if their beliefs

Escape your mental limitations. Don't spend your life being imprisoned by a belief system that limits your potential and prevents your dreams from coming true.

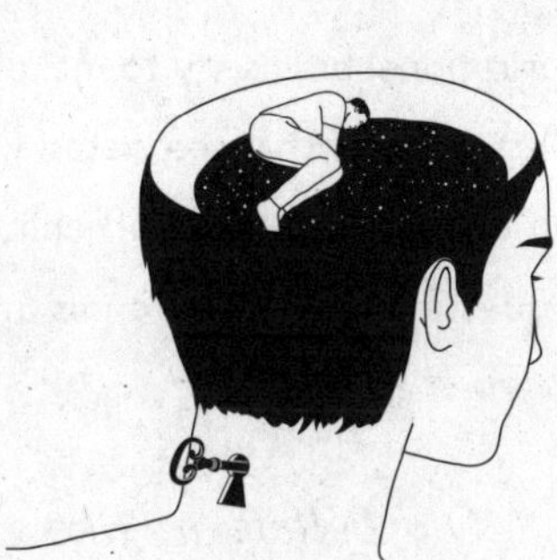

were different from mine. These individuals thought limitlessly. They seemed like positive people, too. They talked about charity, respecting other people, being healthy.

When I started looking at people who'd accomplished some of the greatest achievements on our planet, the theme seemed to be the same. I also studied some of the most admired spiritual leaders. I found many who stated that our beliefs create the life we experience.

I realized that what I'd been taught wasn't necessarily false; it was true for the person who'd told me it and for others around me. When I looked at the lives of those people, there was a common theme: struggle. They had no reason to believe otherwise. Life hadn't treated them well, so all they'd known was hardship.

Our rational brains try to make sense of life around us. If someone offers a theory that resonates, we accept it as our truth. When I was told that life would be difficult, it was much easier to believe than to question it. I took it on as a truth because it fitted with my life experiences so far.

Our beliefs are like a lens we use to view life;
we see what we convince ourselves is true.

With this realization, I knew that if I could change my beliefs, I could change my life. I wanted to know if there were people out there who were born into circumstances like mine but still managed to achieve great things.

Not only were there countless cases of such people, but also many of them were born into worse situations than mine. Reading their success stories disproved everything I'd been conditioned to believe. They helped me to build a solid case against my own rational mind, using evidence. The more stories I read, the firmer my resolve became.

I could now accept a new belief: I can change my future and achieve great things.

The key point here is that if you want to change your belief, you have to *disprove your current belief by finding enough evidence to support the belief you want*. There are always success stories out there that will assist you in this process.

Repeating affirmations

What you verbalize will eventually materialize. You have the power to talk aspects of your reality into existence.

Don't underestimate the power of affirmations. Affirmations are positive statements that describe what you wish to achieve. Simply saying something over and over again, with great conviction, creates a belief deep in our subconscious that this statement is true.

It's visible in everyday society. We're fed certain notions about the world and they're repeated over and over again. For example, a mother who constantly tells her child that they're shy will reinforce this idea in the child's head. The child may not actually feel shy. But, through repetition of this idea, the child might start to believe it. Consequently, the child may grow up to be shy – the mother's words become a self-fulfilling prophecy.

Once again, this leads me to stress the importance of surrounding yourself with people who are feeding you empowering thoughts. This isn't to say that you should only keep friends who say nice things about you. But it does mean that you should pick people who are supportive, not destructive.

If you keep on being told you can't do something, you'll believe you can't.

Repeating affirmations is a conscious process. It's the act of sending instructions to your subconscious mind. Once these beliefs are planted, your subconscious mind will do everything it can to bring these ideas into fruition. It's like writing instructions into a computer program to carry out a process for you. Once the lines of code are in, the program can run automatically to bring the desired result.

From personal experience, reciting statements that I simply cannot trick myself into believing doesn't work effectively. Going back to my example about changing beliefs, I couldn't just tell myself that I could change my future and do big things. I had to find *proof* to challenge my old beliefs rationally.

The same thing should be done before affirming ideas, so that these statements aren't rejected. This is a much more effective way to use affirmations. Adding substance to affirmations before you repeat them gives them greater power.

Maintaining a high vibration is important throughout life, and I find that if you can say your affirmations during a period when you're feeling good, they'll have greater momentum; though repeating affirmations can raise your vibration whatever your mood. Saying something out loud like you really mean it can completely change your state.

Affirmations should be in your own words. Say them in your voice, as if you're telling facts to a friend. Only repeat positive statements – don't recite what you don't want. What we resist often persists, because the energy we exude in avoiding it is also returned to us. So, for example, you might say, 'I have great confidence in everything I do,' rather than, 'I am not nervous anymore.' And affirmations should be spoken in the present tense.

When you act as if the goal is already the truth, your subconscious mind believes that it is and acts accordingly.

The amount of time you spend on your affirmations is entirely up to you. Anything between two and five minutes a day is reasonable. However, emotional investment is more important than duration, so say them like you mean them.

The power of words

Words can hurt, help or heal. There's power in everything you write and say. Your message is significant; be wise with it.

In the 1990s, Dr Masaru Emoto carried out ground-breaking experiments on the impact of emotional energy on water.[11] In one study, he wrote positive and negative words on containers full of water. He then froze samples of the water from each container.

Among the negative words were 'you fool' while a positive one was 'love'. Dr Emoto's thinking was that if our words are energy and water is an absorber of energy, then surely the words would affect the water in some way.

He was absolutely right. The water that had been exposed to positive words formed beautiful ice crystals, with the words 'love'

11 Emoto, M., *The Hidden Messages in Water* (Simon and Schuster, 2005)

and 'gratitude' forming the most stunning ones. In contrast, the water exposed to negative words formed unappealing patterns with distorted shapes. He found the same results by verbally communicating words to different water containers. It was clear that our words carry a vibration.

As I mentioned in Part Two of this book, our bodies are mainly made up of water. Now imagine how much our words might affect us.

Set the intention

If you're unsure about what you want, you'll end up with a lot of things you're unsure of.

Before going after your goals, you have to know what you want. You cannot attain that which you're unsure about. You wouldn't go into a restaurant and say, 'I think I want the vegetable curry,' when placing your order. You either want it or you don't.

If you're confused about your intention, the results that follow will reflect that. For example, if the waiter asks you how spicy you want the vegetable curry but you say you're not sure, you could receive any level of spice. If you then find it too spicy, it would be your own fault because you didn't give clear instructions.

Setting the right goal is everything. It has to reflect what you deeply desire – not what you think you *should* want. For many years, the things I believed I wanted were actually only to impress other people. Sometimes I'd achieve these things and feel surprised that they didn't satisfy me.

Your goals should reflect who you are as a person. They should be the things you think about all the time that you know will improve the quality of your life. Having materialistic desires is fine; only those who have completely transcended their ego don't have any. Nevertheless, your goals should mean a lot to you. For example, someone might want a bigger house to raise a large family in, so they can share good times together. There's greater meaning to this goal than wanting the bigger house just to prove how rich you are.

Once you make an intention clear, the Universe will work in miraculous ways. When we put what we want out there, the manifestation process begins and things start to unfold in our favour. Our dreams come to life.

J. Cole is a renowned American rapper, writer and producer, who previously had jobs in advertising and debt collecting. In a 2011 interview, Cole claimed that after watching the rapper 50 Cent's movie *Get Rich or Die Tryin'*, he was inspired to make himself a T-shirt carrying the bold statement: 'Produce for Jay-Z or Die Tryin''. In the interview, Cole said he thought he could take a different route to becoming a rapper by first becoming noticed as a producer. He wanted to create an avenue to his main goal, and that's why he created the T-shirt.[12]

After wearing the T-shirt in the hope that someone from the music industry or Jay-Z himself would recognize him, it wasn't until several years later that something amazing happened: with his goal set and his great work ethic partnered with self-belief, Cole was contacted by Jay-Z and was later signed to his record label Roc Nation. Cole has now rapped with Jay-Z on several tracks and produced them himself.

12 'J. Cole Interview' (Fuse On Demand, YouTube, January 2011)

Write down your goals

You are the author of your future.
Write about what you desire and live your story.

I once read that if you write down your goals they're more likely to come true. I was intrigued, so I decided to look into it. I began to unravel all these wonderful statistics from studies and remarkable stories of people who wrote down their goals on paper and ended up manifesting them years later.

A popular example is that of the professional American football quarterback Colin Kaepernick. When he was in fourth grade, Kaepernick wrote himself a letter in which he quite accurately predicted that he would become a professional football player, what team he'd play for, and even his weight and height.[13] Colin isn't a psychic; he just knew what he wanted, and he was specific about his vision for the future. His ideas eventually manifested into his reality.

13 Sessler, M., 'Kaepernick foretold future in fourth-grade letter' (NFL.com, 17 December 2012)

When you write down your goals, you turn your intentions into something tangible. Define them in detail, and this will help you to stay focused so you don't lose your way.

I've had great fortune when it comes to writing down my goals. In the past I've written very specific details about my goals and they've manifested exactly how I wrote them. The way I write my goals is quite specific. I'm sharing these details with you here so you can make use of them, too.

Write down your goals with a pen or pencil

The act of writing down your goals on paper, rather than on-screen, creates what I like to think is a magical impression on your mind. When you reread these goals, in your own handwriting, this impression on the mind deepens, giving greater force to your goals.

Be honest

Write them down exactly as you wish them. Don't restrict yourself or write them in a way that you think is 'right'. If you have big goals, that's fine. Thinking big means you're open to receiving big.

Write them in the present tense

Just as with affirmations, write down your goals in the present tense, as if you've already accomplished them, such as 'I am a great mathematician' (if that's what you want to become). Your subconscious mind will choose the path of least resistance in order to manifest your goals.

Make them positive

Remember, always write your goals down from a positive stance: focus on what you want, not what you don't want.

Write them in your own voice

Write them exactly how you'd say them. You don't need to use fancy language. These goals are to be understood by you and you alone. Write them in a way that you connect with easily; you shouldn't have to try to translate them in your head.

Be specific

Write down as many details as you can. The clearer the goal, the clearer the outcome. Remember, the subconscious mind is working from a set of instructions, and the outcome can only be as good as the instructions provided.

If possible, write your goals without a timeframe in mind. Otherwise, when the goal doesn't manifest when you expect it to, you might be disheartened and become doubtful, which lowers your vibration and pushes your goal further away. However, if you're someone who is motivated by pressure, a deadline might help you to go into action. It's your call: if a timeframe would be helpful, include one. If not, don't.

Set goals you feel confident about. The best way to build confidence is to start with smaller goals. Once you manifest them, you'll be confident about bigger goals manifesting, too.

Once you've identified and written down your goals, say them out loud every day. If you need to make small adjustments to them, then do so. However, changing them drastically and frequently is almost like planting a new seed each time, so keep that in mind. You need to know what you want.

Imagine it to live it

What becomes real in your mind
will become real in your life.

Visualization is the process of creating an experience or intention in your mind, before you have it in your life.

Global superstar Arnold Schwarzenegger has made several references to visualizing his goals before he actually achieved them. Michael Jordan, the legendary basketball player, claims that he visualized the type of player he wanted to become before he found success. In fact, top athletes often use visualization. One of the best tennis players ever to grace our planet, Roger Federer, says he uses it in his training regime. These sportsmen are training and performing to perfection – within their minds.

Psychologists Alan Budley, Shane Murphy and Robert Woolfolk suggested in their 1994 book that mental practice results in better performance than not physically practising at all.[14] The brain patterns that are activated when you *imagine* an action are very similar to those that are activated when you physically perform the action, so visualization can actually train your brain for the event.

When we visualize what we desire, not only do we align ourselves to vibrate on the same frequency as the object of our visualization, but we also influence our subconscious mind in the same way as we do with affirmations.

The brain and the nervous system cannot tell the difference between what is imagined and what is real.

We can take advantage of this. If our brain believes that the ideas we're feeding it are true, then our life will begin to reflect that, too. If you imagine yourself to be more confident than you currently are and the brain thinks it's true, you'll be more confident!

14 Budney, A., Murphy, S. and Woolfolk, R., 'Imagery and Motor Performance: What Do We Really Know?', Sheikh, A., Korn., E. (Eds), *Imagery in Sports and Physical Performance* (Baywood, 1994)

Engage your senses

When we talk about visualization as a process, we don't mean creating single mental images. You have to create scenes, not pictures. In those scenes you must involve all your senses: taste, sight, touch, smell and hearing.

Go into as much detail as you can. For example, if you want a new car, don't just picture the car. Put yourself in the car, driving it around. Think about how you feel while driving it; the sound of the car; the sight of other cars on the road; the temperature of the air around you, and so on. Live the experience as if it were true in that precise moment. Get creative with your scenes. Really bring them to life by making them bright, colourful, loud and big. All you need to do is close your eyes and start creating.

It's important to create a scene that makes you feel good. Your imagination should ignite positive emotions, and this requires a lot of focus, so always do it in a quiet place where you can relax and distance yourself from any distractions.

> *When I use this technique, I get confirmation that I'm doing it effectively when I start to feel a little tingly. That is, I begin*

to feel as if it is actually happening and it fills me with excitement.

If you find it hard to create visuals in your head, there are things you can do to help yourself. Vision boards are very popular. Collect pictures and clippings that depict what you want to manifest and fix them to a board. This will help you clarify your goals, and you can place the board in an obvious place in your home to keep you focused on your intentions.

I like to keep a vision board as well as practise visualization. I don't keep a physical board, but collect images on a personal website and try to spend a few minutes viewing it every day. This has worked well for me. I even manifested my dream proposal to my life partner by gathering images on Pinterest, a popular vision board platform, of how I wanted it to look.

As a teenager, I used to produce music as a hobby. I was a big fan of a group called So Solid Crew, one of the biggest acts around at the time. I had their logo printed onto my school pencil case. In class, I daydreamed about working with them.

A year or two later, a member of So Solid Crew, known as Swiss, released an album called *Pain 'n' Musiq*. I absolutely fell in love with this album and would listen to it day and night. It put me in a trance and I'd visualize myself working with Swiss and creating great music together.

Remarkably, it wasn't long after this that I did have the chance to work with Swiss; through a musical artist and mentor of mine called Clive, who happened to be friends with him. Eventually the three of us collaborated on a few songs, before just Swiss and I worked together.

The Universe is supporting you

Don't worry about how it's going to happen, otherwise you'll begin to create limitations. Just be certain about what you want and the entire Universe will rearrange itself for you. Whatever the path you might be on right now, it will support you. It will provide you with the signs to get you to where you want to be.

The 13th-century poet Rumi wrote: 'The Universe is not outside you. Look inside yourself; everything that you want, you already are.' Rumi may also have agreed that the only reason the Universe might not be available to you is if you're not attuned to it. The Universe already exists within you, but it's not perceivable to you if you're not vibrating high enough. However, you can bring it to light through your words, actions, emotions and beliefs.

The Universe helps us to create, or rather, to bring possibilities into our reality. It gives you signs to follow and sends you ideas to act on. It's up to you to respond.

You might decide your goal is to work for yourself at something you enjoy. Then one day you randomly think of a specific idea, like selling your food recipes online. If you don't think much of it, you probably won't act on it; you'll probably just dismiss it as a passing thought.

In the following weeks, you might start coming across bloggers sharing their own recipes. This seems coincidental, so you continue to ignore the signs and instead invest your efforts elsewhere. But by ignoring the signs, you could be missing out on everything you want. Sometimes, we ignore the signs because we think we're supposed to achieve our goals in a particular way.

All I really wanted to do was utilize my creative skills to change the world in a positive way – and, of course, live comfortably. I used to think that the only avenue for this was clothing. Once I let go of the idea of *how* it was going to happen, I found myself trying out other ideas. Seemingly casual thoughts led me to where I am now. I trust where they'll take me next, knowing they'll bring me closer to where I want to be.

These days, when terms like the Law of Attraction are thrown around, people assume that your dreams will manifest without any effort on your part. But you must take action on the thoughts and ideas that crop up in your mind; the inspiration that the Universe sends you. They're nudges from the Universe saying, 'Go this way! Try this!'

Intention without action is just a wish. A goal only comes to life when you decide to pursue it. The Universe is always supporting you, but you must be willing to do your part in the manifestation process.

PART SIX

Manifesting Goals: Taking Action

Introduction

It's not about where you're at. It's about what you're doing *about where you're at.*

I believe in taking action and building momentum towards your goal. This shouldn't be confused with taking big steps; you can move forward with baby steps. However, it's always a good idea to give everything you've got.

For example, if my intention is to be the biggest music artist in the world, I don't have to try to sell out arenas right away. I could start by creating a song. That's a small step in the right direction.

At the same time, I could pour every little part of me into the song. I could ensure the lyrics are the best they can be and I can perform the vocals to the best of my abilities. This might mean that I have to spend extra time on it, or learn new skills, but that's all an investment into my future – my dreams.

Many of us have a series of excuses ready to explain why something can't be done. Often, you'll hear people relay their doubts or explain how they lack time, expertise, resources, money, etc. But when we want a goal badly enough, we make sacrifices in other areas to make it possible. I've come to realize that it's not necessary to have lots of free time to achieve a dream. The same goes for money and other resources. What you do need is a vision, a belief in it, and serious dedication. You'll find a way if you keep taking action.

We might not want to sacrifice our luxuries or undergo the pain of hard work to get our desired outcome. We don't want to step outside of our comfort zone. We accept mediocrity while we simultaneously complain about it. But then that outcome will remain out of reach. 'I'm not ready,' we say. But when *will* you be ready? Sir Richard Branson was diagnosed as dyslexic at school. He dropped out at the age of 16 to start a magazine. He was hardly 'ready' in most people's eyes. But he was driven.

He didn't know anything about planes, but he started Virgin Atlantic anyway. Along with an incredible net worth, Richard Branson's Virgin Group includes more than 400 companies. He's as driven today as he was when he was 16. He isn't lucky; his history reveals bad trades throughout. He's just someone who believes in his vision and he acts on it.

Change requires action

Once, I needed money to clear a debt. I set my vibration high and ensured I was feeling good. But I didn't take action. I just expected money to come to me.

During this time, I won a free watch in an online competition. I didn't usually enter competitions because I'd never won anything in the past, but I was feeling optimistic and so I entered. I was grateful that I won the watch, but it wasn't what I needed at this time. I needed money.

As time dragged on, the money I needed didn't appear and I began to get disheartened. I was certain it was going to come, so why didn't it? Well, you see: I hadn't noticed the opportunity the Universe had given me to take action. I'd won a prize and I didn't consider that it could help me on my way. Yes – I could have sold it! As soon as I realized my mistake, I *did* sell it, and made the money I needed to pay off my debt.

Sometimes, steps towards your goals come disguised as opportunities to take action. If you don't take action, you'll miss out on the reward. Expecting change to happen when you don't change anything yourself is like making chocolate raspberry cake in the exact same way, every single day, and expecting it to turn into a chocolate strawberry cake. If you don't add strawberries to the cake instead of raspberries, then it won't change! It sounds a bit silly and obvious, right? But so many people go through their lives expecting change when they're doing the same things every day. They feed all this positive energy via their thoughts, words and emotions, but take no action, which is vibratory in itself.

The easy route

I find that a lot people know what to do, but they still don't do it. They rely on justification or an easier solution because the real solution seems too long-winded. Some people would rather use their energy to find a way to use less effort for the same result. Working smarter is essential for effective productivity, but even finding a solution to work smarter requires a lot of effort. We must come to terms with the idea that some things have to be done the *difficult* way.

For example, if you want to lose weight, you have to create a calorie deficit by either increasing physical activity, improving your diet, or both. Most people know they need to do these things but they don't commit to them. Instead, they'll look for a magic pill or another shortcut to solve their problem. They spend excessive time, energy and money on trying out different miracle cures, when they could have achieved much more if they simply decided to apply some effort.

Other people in this situation may do nothing at all. They want to lose weight and they'll moan about it, but they don't take any action. Many of us will label these people as lazy. People usually act in this way because of two things. One is that they simply don't believe that they can achieve the results that they want to, so they're defeated by the idea of it straight away. The second is that they find the idea of working for the result too painful. People won't want to take action on things if they perceive the process of achieving the results as being too hard. The idea of going to the gym or eating healthily may seem much more painful than remaining how they are. So these people take no action. They tend to stick with easier and more comfortable options – but rarely do we grow within our comfort zone.

Sadly, many will wait until they have no other option before they commit to changes, when you see your current situation as being more painful than going through whatever it takes to get what you desire. Great pain and pressure can force great changes to occur. This is the same reason why people will put up with toxic relationships until they reach breaking point. They may find the idea of being single and lonely more daunting than putting up with their abusive partner.

Step out of your comfort zone
and face your fears. Growth takes
place when you are challenged,
not when you are comfortable.

If you want something enough, you'll take action on it. But don't wait for your pain threshold to be tested. This will only delay results in the manifestation process. Start asking yourself how badly you want to achieve your goals. Do you want them more than you fear the process of getting there?

Consistency leads to results

We must be consistent as we strive to achieve our goals.

Imagine that you want to build lean muscle, so you purchase a three-month workout and nutrition plan from a personal trainer. You then follow 50 per cent of the instructions, but after a month you notice that you're not getting the results you'd hoped for. You might conclude that the plan doesn't work. Alternatively, you might follow the whole plan but observe after two or three weeks that the results aren't showing. Again, you say that the plan doesn't work. In both cases, you simply give up on it.

If you do 50 per cent of the plan, you can expect no more than 50 per cent of the results. If you're not consistent in your actions, then you can't assume that you'll see the final results you were expecting. I myself did a home workout series. It was a two-month programme and after a month I couldn't see any exciting results. In spite of this, I promised myself I'd see it out until the end. I'm glad I did: I dropped nearly three inches off my waist by the end of the second month.

The same goes for meditation, affirmations, visualizations and any other positive practice. If you want to reap the benefits, you have to do regular, solid practice. Be committed to the cause. With consistency, we can create habits that shape our lives.

Lack of time isn't an excuse. If you can't make the time for something, it's not a high enough priority for you. If something is important to you, you'll make the time for it.

'We are what we repeatedly do.
Excellence then, is not an act, but a habit.'

ARISTOTLE

Soccer legend David Beckham was once known for his amazing free kicks. Each time he stepped up to take one, the crowd were certain that the ball was going to land in the back of the net.

Beckham didn't become a master of free kicks overnight. He practised over and over again. He didn't practise until he got his free kicks right, but until he couldn't get them wrong. Even when he was scoring them, he ensured that he stayed consistent with his practice. With repetition comes habit.

Not everything will work, or be the best fit, for you. Reviewing your methods and adapting to change is vital. If you've given something a good shot but you're still not progressing, this might be a sign that you need to try a new approach. Use your intuition to guide you. If something feels wrong, it usually is!

Ordinary or extraordinary?

The difference between ordinary and extraordinary is simple: extraordinary people will get things done even when they don't feel like it, because they're fully committed to their goals.

When you pursue a goal you're passionate about, you'll naturally be motivated to achieve it. If you don't find the process enjoyable, then you may want to reevaluate where you're investing your efforts.

This isn't to say that you won't have your down days, even if you're very focused on your goal. If you hold a high vibration or make an effort to increase it, motivation will come quite easily to you, but the prospect of having to take action can lower your vibration if you're not in the right frame of mind.

Maintaining your motivation isn't always an easy task, especially following a setback or on a dark and gloomy day. Motivation comes and goes. Low motivation might indicate that you need time out to recharge. Or it could mean you need to go out and search for inspiration.

If you *still* don't feel motivated, proceed anyway and be willing to get things done. You didn't expect me to say that, did you? It might not sound very appealing, but experience has taught me that this behaviour – this *grit* – is a key difference between ordinary and extraordinary. It's about commitment. When you don't want to roll out of bed in the early hours, or when you really can't be bothered to go to that meeting on the other side of town – you do it anyway! You recognize that the effort you put in will be worth the rewards that come later.

Although writing is a passion of mine, I'll readily admit that I've groaned at some of the tasks involved in creating this book. Some have been extremely tedious – but even as I write this line, I'm focused on the result.

Things are always easier when you're in the mood to do them, but if you want to live a greater life than the average person, you have to commit the same effort even when you're not.

Procrastination will delay your dreams

Procrastination is a habit. If the task ahead of you seems so insurmountable that you don't know where to start, you'll put it off – again and again; perhaps you choose a distraction as being more favourable or comfortable. It's important to kill this habit if you want to manifest your goals. Do it before procrastination becomes the assassination of your dreams.

Behaviours of chronic procrastinators include:

- putting things off until a later date or the last minute
- carrying out less urgent tasks before urgent ones
- getting distracted before or while doing something
- facing things only when they're unavoidable

- claiming that you haven't got time to do something
- waiting for the right time or mood to do something
- not completing tasks at all

Does this sound like you? Procrastinators avoid things that require action. Some of us do everything apart from what we need to do in order to be in harmony with our goals. For example, when typing up an essay for a deadline, a procrastinator might first browse the Internet and waste precious time.

We don't just procrastinate over small tasks, but over our biggest goals, too. My friend Tony's mentoring client, Malcolm, is a clear example of someone who procrastinated before taking action on his dreams. Malcolm was fearful, unwilling to leave his comfort zone, and overanalytical. These are common traits in chronic procrastinators. These qualities led him to deviate from the path to achieving his goals.

The story with Malcolm began when he first went to see Tony for support to reach his goal – something he really wanted: to start his own business. It would need his full-time commitment, which meant he'd have to leave his current job.

Malcolm feared what he couldn't understand, which was how he would make a viable income with his business idea. He lacked self-belief. He doubted his own potential and he didn't want to feel uncomfortable by compromising his existing lifestyle. He told himself that he was being unrealistic, so he hadn't pursued his passion.

After Tony had set Malcolm on the path to starting his business, Malcolm suddenly convinced himself that he didn't have enough information to get it going. He felt that he needed to do more research, which required more time. He believed this because, again, he feared failure.

Research is, of course, crucial if you intend to start a successful business, so his intentions were reasonable. The problem was that he *did* have all the information he needed; he was using an imagined need for further research as an excuse to delay taking action. Malcolm was eager to start his own business, and he believed it would add value to the world, but sadly he lacked the confidence to take the leap and get started.

After spending months researching every detail of his plans, Malcolm concluded that his idea was pointless. He wrote it off completely. He'd managed to talk himself out of it. This came as a shock to Tony, because he could see that Malcolm's idea had great potential and that he was committed to it.

But this wasn't the end. Time went by and Malcolm's job was made redundant. Instead of finding another employer, Malcolm decided to invest his redundancy money into his thoroughly researched business idea. This time he had no choice but to make it work; he needed an income to live on.

With a bit of capital to work with and no other option, Malcolm finally took action. His business eventually became a success. If he hadn't been made redundant and received his payout, he might never have started his business. Now Malcolm realizes that he was held back by fear and wishes he'd started his business earlier.

> *You don't need it all figured out. The more you think you do, the more you'll procrastinate and fear moving forward. Have courage and start now, even if you start small. Just go for it!*

When you find yourself procrastinating, it's important to devise a strategy to overcome this. It's easy to do this for smaller goals, like completing an essay, but it's more challenging with bigger goals, like creating a successful online business.

So break your goals down. Big goals can be overwhelming, and it's hard to imagine how you'll ever cross the finish line. It's more effective to set smaller goals and prioritize them in order of urgency.

If the goals still seem big after you've made them smaller, break them down further.

If you can meet smaller goals, you'll become more confident about bigger goals. Even if you're trying to manifest money, start by making the goal a fraction of the desired amount. So, if the goal is to have £10,000, work on making £100 to begin with. After you make £100, you can try to make another £100 until you reach your target amount.

We have four types of feel-good hormones in our body: dopamine, serotonin, oxytocin and endorphins. Dopamine, in particular, encourages us to take action towards our goals and provides us with feelings of pleasure when we achieve them. When we lack enthusiasm for a task, it means our dopamine levels are low.

When you break big goals down into smaller ones, you overcome this. Your brain will celebrate every time you meet a goal by releasing dopamine. You'll then be encouraged to take further action on the rest of your goals.

If your final goal is time-sensitive, make sure each smaller goal has a deadline on it. You can only meet big goals on time if your smaller ones are done on time, too.

If you still struggle to beat procrastination, try the following techniques:

1. **Get rid of every distraction possible**, even if this means changing your environment. Have you ever been hungry and ended up snacking on something unhealthy just because it was there? If it wasn't there, the temptation wouldn't exist. We get distracted by things that are easily available to us.

2. **Give yourself an incentive to complete the task.** For example, tell yourself you can meet with your friends later if you finish whatever needs to be done. This will give you something to look forward to and motivate you to take action.

3. **Take breaks to do something enjoyable.** We all need a little time out when working, but make sure your breaks are for a fixed duration. If you want to watch a new episode of a show, schedule a period for it and don't exceed it.

4. **Get creative.** Make your tasks more appealing. When doing activities that don't require much thought, you could play

music in the background. This will raise your vibration. Singing along might make the activity even more enjoyable.

5. **Get some help if required.** Never be afraid to ask for help. Talk to someone who's recently accomplished a similar goal to you. This may provide much-needed inspiration and they may be able to give you valuable guidance.

6. **Give yourself a consequence for not taking action.** For example, you could tell yourself that if you don't go to the gym today, you can't watch television for the entire week. To ensure you don't go back on what you say, make sure you tell others about it. This leads me to my final point...

7. **Announce your intentions to some trustworthy friends.** This will give you some accountability; they'll know if you don't stick to your plans, and they might even give you a little push to ensure that you achieve what you set out to do.

The quick-fix society

Patience is a must when pursuing your goals. Your desires can take a while to manifest. If you believe you're doing everything in your power to manifest your goals, sometimes all you need to do is practise a little patience. Accept today as it is and stay optimistic in the face of delays, setbacks or challenges.

Time is the most precious commodity you have. When time is spent, it's gone forever. This is why businesses that save their customers time often thrive. But while these companies might significantly improve our lives, they've also contributed to the creation of a quick-fix society.

The quick-fix society demands instant solutions. We expect things to be done straight away. We want to use less effort and less time to get a desirable outcome. Online clothing retailers will get clothes to us the next day. Services like Amazon Prime get all manner of goods to us within a day. If you want to watch a movie or a television show, you can just hop on to Netflix and pick something. If you want a date, you just need to swipe through a dating app. Meals can be replaced by frozen ones that can be heated in a microwave in a few minutes. No more need for patience – we can get what we want without delay.

There's nothing wrong with indulging in these things now and then, but they've created a culture of impatience. We don't want to wait, and if we have to wait we may lose faith in our intentions. The assumption is that things must arrive quickly, with minimal effort. Don't get me wrong: if you can achieve something great at lightning speed, that's fantastic. Just don't be oblivious to the fact that most things in life require effort and patience.

This quick-fix way of life encourages us to give up on our goals when they don't manifest as rapidly as we'd hoped, and move on to the next thing. This will never be fulfilling. A lot of the time, your goals aren't eluding you; you either haven't put in the effort you need to or you're expecting things to happen instantaneously. Practise a little patience.

You'll get the job, the partner, the house, the car, etc. Just don't rush the process; trust it. You have to grow into your dreams.

Swap short-term pleasures for long-term gains

You're not missing out on anything great if you're using that time to make your life greater.

These days, I tend to party only when there's something to celebrate. But in my late teens and early twenties, I went to a lot of clubs in a lot of places. I even flew all the way to Cancún in Mexico from the UK just to experience the infamous American spring break. I was living for the moment. This is important because, as we've learned, we only ever have this current moment and we should enjoy it. But a healthy balance between living for the moment and investing in the future is always required when you have goals.

When I was working in an office, every Friday I used to get that feeling of excitement because I knew I was going to celebrate a weekend free from work. I began living for the weekend, even though I knew there was more to life. The weekend was the time to reward myself. I'd get intoxicated and spend my hard-earned money in nightclubs. In the moment, when I was drunk, I felt great!

But this is what my actions were really saying:

> *Look at me! I'm working for hours on end in a job I don't really like, for someone who doesn't respect me. Therefore, I'm living for the weekend, to celebrate my freedom and spend my hard-earned cash on overpriced lethal substances that come in fancy bottles. This way I can feel better about life for a moment, by escaping the reality I face during the working week while impressing people who might be in a similar predicament.*

Deep down, I was always wondering when my life would start to resemble my vision of having my own business, doing something I loved. I expected it to transform by pure chance.

I'd continually complain that I had no money to put towards my dreams. It was ironic, but I know I'm not alone. People often complain that they don't have the time or the money to start their own business, while simultaneously spending lots of time and money on leisure activities. In some places, a single glass of an alcoholic beverage costs more than a book. Which one is more likely to change your life? People invest in the wrong places, and often they unwittingly fund someone else's dreams; someone who's worked their ass off and has now manifested their goals thanks to your spare cash.

There are so many individuals living like I was. And if it's not partying, it's something else. Yes, we should enjoy our lives and make the most of every moment. However, giving up what you want most for what you want *now* can deprive you of life's real treasures.

I believe that everyone is destined for a greater life. Yet I understand that many people are unwilling to delay brief gratification for the sake of long-term rewards. When you're unwilling to delay temporary pleasures, this can have massive implications for your future.

Most people are living the 'When I have X, I'll be happy' way of life, but this is a delusion. However, you can have pleasure in the present by living mindfully, appreciatively, and altering your perspective.

You're free to make your own choices, but you can't escape their consequences. Sometimes we have to sacrifice small things to get our hands on the bigger blessings in life.

I'm not saying you should ignore all of your urges or stop having fun. But form a healthy balance between work and play while moderating where you're placing your time and energy.

Faith vs fear

No matter how much you worry, your problem isn't going to improve. Be wiser with your attention and energy. You can only step up in the world once you put your anxieties, fears and worries under your feet.

Faith is an active choice we make to stay optimistic. It can be extremely demanding to show faith in your goals at times. Fear will creep in and deceive you. It will steer you away from all the greatness that you're due to be blessed with.

Fear is a mechanism that helps us to avoid physical harm or death. Yet we often use it to stay comfortable – to avoid challenges. We utilize it in the wrong way and it just ends up hindering our progress and preventing us from reaching our full potential. Fear keeps our lives mediocre, because it forces us to flee from our potential, rather than from anything truly harmful. Fear sets us back in our everyday lives and controls our choices. We use our precious energy to imagine what could go wrong, instead of having faith in what could go right. And our actions reflect this.

Both faith and fear ask you to believe in something that cannot be seen. You may fear stepping outside in the cold because you believe it will make you ill, even if at present you're not ill and it's unlikely that exposure to cold would cause illness. This is just a figment of your imagination until it manifests as your reality.

We make fear-based assumptions all the time. Unfortunately, when we feed these assumptions they expand into our experience.

Fear is a low vibrational state and it therefore brings about more of what you *don't* want in your life. Unlike faith, it disempowers the mind and this is reflected in your experiences. If you remove fear, your experience improves. For example, a surgeon without fear is likely to be less hesitant and more focused. Their decision-making may be considerably better, resulting in an improved performance.

Replacing fear with faith encourages us to do the unthinkable: it helps us to explore the realms of possibility. Faith doesn't necessarily make things easier, but it does make them possible. When going after your goals, you must have an unwavering faith that can remain sturdy when challenged by venomous opinions or unfortunate twists of fate. The faith I'm talking about is the one that says, 'I'm going to win,' when all you can see is losses.

Sometimes all we have is our faith – our faith in the fact that things are going to get better. Hang on to it and keep believing, even if that means you're the only one who does.

Flow with the Universse

Embrace good vibes and learn to let things flow. There is no need to force outcomes. Once you are in harmony with the Universe, what's meant to be yours will come to you.

No one in the world has always manifested every single goal they've wanted in the time they've desired. You can change outcomes through your vibe, but you must accept that things will unfold in their own time and for your highest good – which sometimes means in a way you hadn't imagined.

Once you've learned to hone your manifestation skills, you must let go of your attachment to the goal. By trying to force or control the outcome, you breed resistance by feeding fear and doubt. When your heart is in something, only good things can follow.

Now, this may not always seem true. But remember that rejections are just redirections to better things. Setbacks are pauses for thought, opportunities to alter your plans – for the better. And however big any failure may feel at the time, there's *always* a lesson to learn. Only with faith can we recognize the value of our apparent downfalls. What we truly want often comes wrapped in different packaging.

Learn to let go and let things flow. As I mentioned at the beginning of this book, the concepts of action and inaction must be balanced. Your job is to do the best you can to achieve this.

PART SEVEN

Pain and Purpose

Introduction

Life doesn't battle you because you're weak, it battles you because you're strong. It knows that if it gives you pain, you'll realize your power.

The great Greek philosopher Aristotle claimed that everything happens for a reason. You can apply this when you consider that every experience in your life is designed to shape you and help you grow into the highest and mightiest version of yourself. This means that even a negative experience can be seen as an opportunity for growth, rather than a time for suffering. (This doesn't mean that we shouldn't grieve or feel down when we do go through painful life experiences, and it's important to give yourself time to heal after such events.) If you always play the victim when something goes wrong, life will always treat you like one. Don't let your circumstances define your future.

Aristotle's belief may make people think, 'Yes! I feel that!', give them hope or slightly annoy them. I understand why some might find the phrase irritating; when someone goes through a horrific experience it's very difficult to see reason for it. All they feel is pain, and they may feel that by saying this, you're demonstrating your ignorance about their situation.

However, the majority of us go through at least one period in our lives that we find very tough. So we can relate to someone's low points to some extent, even if we don't understand them exactly, because we have felt low ourselves.

Sometimes we just have to believe there's a good reason behind it that will reveal itself to us when we're ready to acknowledge it.

A schoolteacher of mine once told me a story about how his brother missed the last train from the town he was studying in to go home for the holiday season. When the brother missed the train, he was devastated and angry with himself.

However, later that evening he learned that train he was meant to have taken had tragically crashed and nearly all the passengers had died. Upon hearing this, he thanked God for saving him from what could have been his last breath, and he said, 'Everything happens for

Just because you can't see the
point behind a challenging time,
doesn't mean there isn't one.

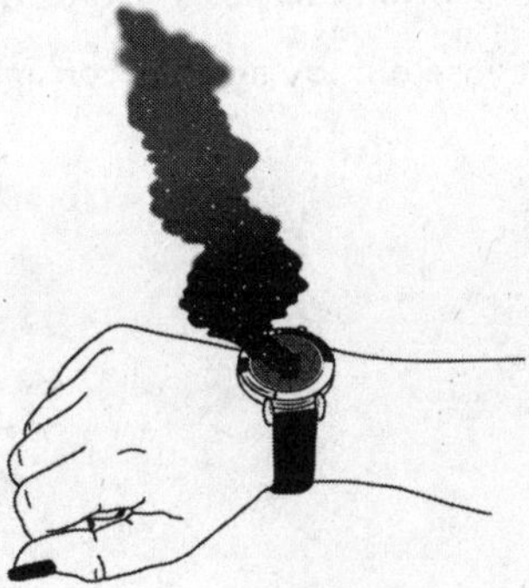

a reason.' I'm sure the friends and family of the deceased passengers wouldn't have agreed, but from the brother's perspective the phrase made perfect sense.

If it hadn't been for my father's death early in my life, I wouldn't be sitting here trying to inspire people; I'd have entirely different stories to tell because my experiences would've been different. This doesn't make the fact that he's gone any better; with my father around, I might have avoided many of my hardships. But the phrase gives you an empowering perspective so you can move forward with your life.

The past cannot be changed; only our perception of it can. By creating this shift in mindset, we start to trust that everything that happens *to* us also happens *for* us. As we begin to change our perception to a positive one, our life improves. If we don't change it, we lose our joy and are consigned to low vibrational states.

Pain changes people

Life will test you
just before it will bless you.

Some of the best changes in life result from the most painful experiences. We need to experience low points in our life in order to gain the wisdom, strength and knowledge we need to appreciate the high points.

When we experience low points on our journey towards change, life can feel confusing and challenging. It's extremely difficult to trust the process and to have faith that good things will follow. But we need to remember that, using the lessons we learn along the way, we can make better choices going forward. If you've had your heart broken before, you might decide to pay more attention when picking a partner. This might lead you down the path to finding your soulmate – someone who treats you much better than anyone ever has before.

Every choice you make leads to more choices. As you go about your day-to-day life, remember that if you make just one different choice, you may experience a completely different day. Imagine a boy going to meet a girl at the cinema for their first date. The boy decides to eat something before he goes, and consequently his stomach becomes unsettled. He then has to visit the bathroom and ends up leaving late for the date. The girl gets tired of waiting and leaves the cinema a few minutes before he arrives.

As he arrives at the cinema and realizes that she's gone, he heads back home, only to bump accidentally into a girl whom he has an instant attraction to. Now imagine they both get talking, fall in love, get married and have kids. All this occurs purely because he missed his actual date.

Everything is connected. If something tragic has happened in your past, think of something good that's happened recently – they're linked. That first event somehow created different choices in you, which led to you experiencing something good.

Sometimes we have to take a look back at the events in our life and start connecting the dots. There was probably a reason for each occurrence. If we look carefully, things might start making sense. If they do, surely we can be certain that all future events, whether they bring us pain or pleasure, have a purpose.

Lessons will repeat themselves

Life conditions you. It swings at you, it kicks you while you're down and it stamps on you. And yet you survive and walk around as the new and improved version of yourself. Because the challenges that some people still find hard, you have overcome.

The next time you pray for your situation to change, realize that you're in that situation so that *you* can change. Life provides us with lessons that we can handle and that will bring out the best in us. It then tests us to make sure we've learned our lesson. Some of these tests are cruel and some are quite lenient.

Occasionally we experience the same obstacles over and over again, because we still have learning to do. It might be that we haven't learned our lesson properly. The best way to confirm if someone has learned their lesson is to test them more than once, further down the line. I could give you a lesson now, and as it would still be fresh in your mind, you'd probably be able to pass a test on it quite easily.

However, if I gave you the same test a few months later, it would be more challenging. This would be a true test of whether or not you have understood what you've been taught. For example, if you rush a relationship with someone you hardly know and then end up getting hurt, the lesson might be that you need to get to know someone before you jump into a relationship with them.

Just saying *that you've learned your lesson is not always enough – you have to* prove *it.*

So the Universe might then introduce you to someone else, someone who has irresistible charm. To prove that you've learned your lesson, you have to show it. If you jump into another relationship quickly, then there's a chance you might get hurt again. While you should take this example lightly, I hope you can see that sometimes we're given the same test more than once, and it can be even harder the second or third time round.

Notice the warning signs

You don't get into a car immediately worrying that you're going to have a crash. That would be a very fearful way to live life and it would drive you insane. However, you could still take measures, such as wearing a seatbelt, to prevent serious injury if an accident did happen. This action, too, may result from fear, but this is why fear exists: to protect us from danger.

If you caused a car accident because you consumed too much alcohol but you survived, it would be even more irresponsible for you to do it again. If you did, you'd be volunteering for another accident, which could potentially lead to your death. In other words, you're ignoring the lesson and suggesting to the Universe that you should receive that lesson again.

So pay attention to the warning signs. You're always being guided by the Universe to live authentically and purposefully, and to experience the greater things in life. But if something doesn't go the way you wanted, ask yourself what you can learn from it – because every bad experience has a learning outcome to be taken on board. Ask yourself what changes you need to make. And don't mask unhealthy choices with optimism when you know they're not right, or let emotional cravings and temporary comfort inspire you to venture for more pain.

If you keep taking a bite out of the cake that harmed you, you no longer fall victim to it, you become a hungry volunteer.

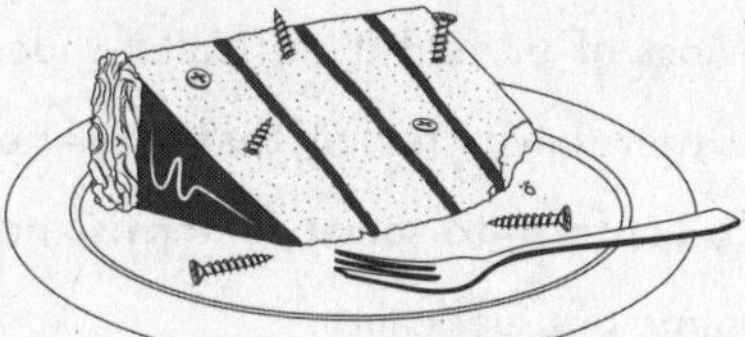

Your higher purpose

You came here loaded with potential, ability, gifts, wisdom, love and intelligence to share with the world. You are here to make the world a better place. You have a purpose, and until you start living it you will have a void inside of you; a feeling you can't quite explain, but that knows that you are meant for more.

I believe that everyone has a purpose in life: a purpose to be of service to the world. This purpose, along with the experience of unconditional love and joy, is the reason for our existence. Purpose provides us with meaning.

Most of us find it difficult to identify what our true purpose is. Others have a feeling that they know what it is, but are often forced to conform to society's norms and reject their real purpose in the name of practicality.

Think of a soccer ball. The purpose of this ball is to be kicked. If the ball just sits there doing nothing in the corner of a room, its purpose is being ignored – however, it doesn't care, because it has no soul. Imagine now that the ball has a soul, giving the ball self-awareness. If the ball stayed sitting in the corner of the room, it would have a strange feeling inside of it, like something was missing. The ball may never find fulfilment because it would probably feel as if it hasn't shown the world its true worth.

Now imagine someone finally picks up the ball and decides to throw it around. As the ball glides through the air, it feels ecstatic. But moments later, the ball feels a void inside itself again, because although it had fun, it wasn't enough.

The ball might then be used in a variety of ways, seeing plenty of action but still feel unfulfilled. The ball assumes that the more events that occur in its life, the closer it'll come to fulfilment. But the more events it experiences, the more this idea is disproved.

Until one day, when the ball is *kicked*. In this moment, everything makes sense to the ball. It understands what it was designed for: it was supposed to be kicked. It looks back at the events that have already taken place and starts connecting the dots. When it was being moved through the air, and when it felt someone applying pressure to it, it experienced feelings of excitement that related to its purpose. The ball now knows what it's been searching for all along.

We gain a modicum of satisfaction from applying ourselves to roles that aren't our own profound purpose, but rarely do we have lasting satisfaction. That's not to say that you can't experience joy – after all, we can always raise our vibration. But we can only feel ultimate fulfilment if we meet the purpose we were made for.

You may find the idea of having a higher purpose to be far-fetched, but if you found a smartphone in the middle of a field, you'd assume that someone had dropped it there. You wouldn't think that something so complex was formed naturally by events in nature, over millions of years, without having a designer. Yet we believe the whole human race, which is far more complex than a smartphone, was produced by a series of mutations and survival of the fittest.

Many of us seem to accept that we have no purpose in life, and that we're each just another human being in this Universe of billions upon billions of galaxies. However, just like a smartphone, there must surely be a purpose in your existence.

When people go through their lives without really believing in a higher purpose, they're not making the most of their existence.

These individuals could go through their whole life just trying to make ends meet. Their purpose in life will always be driven by daily survival, the need to pay the next bill. Of course, bills do matter. We need to pay for food, water, shelter, clothing and utilities. But do you honestly believe you were put on this planet just to exist in such a manner and then die? Do you truly believe that life is simply about making money?

Life is greater if you live with purpose.
When you find a meaningful reason for
doing what you do, you will feel complete.

Just like I used to, many people spend their days working at a job that means nothing to them and living for their two days of freedom each week. During those two days, they'll either do very little or go on a spending spree to make the most of that freedom – as I did by going to a club every weekend. Every week they'll look forward to those two days, wishing their precious time away because they want their time away from work – their 'free time' – to come quicker. The result is that a whole life can go by in a flash.

Life is often difficult and money does give us much more freedom. Nevertheless, have faith that you can serve a purpose for humankind and also meet your financial needs. This purpose doesn't have to be something huge – you don't have to be the next Dalai Lama or even the next Mark Zuckerberg. However, you must seek to add value, and the only way to do this is by doing something you enjoy with all of your heart. This is why passion plays such a big part in living a great life.

Not everyone knows what they're passionate about. Spiritual medium Darryl Anka claims to channel a being known as Bashar, who advises that following your 'excitement' is the shortest path to realizing what you want; your next step should always be the one you find most exciting. You don't need to justify it, says Bashar, you just need to do it.[15]

So take action on whatever it is that truly excites you. Make sure you don't choose something that you label as exciting because you can't think of anything else, or because you think other people will see it as exciting.

The things that you're naturally drawn towards aren't random; they're picking you out in the same way that you're pursuing them. It really is as simple as this.

15 'Bashar: Finding your Highest Excitement' (New Realities, YouTube, 26 September 2006)

So don't overcomplicate it by thinking that you need to have it all figured out. And don't be dishonest with yourself and force action on something you feel is unfeasible. For example, if you really like drawing, you could start by creating a website or social media account and sharing some of your work with the world. Don't try to sell your drawings for thousands of pounds right away, particularly if this seems like a long shot to you at this stage. It should be something you're willing to do for free, without any expectation, because it's something you're truly passionate about. If it doesn't excite you, it's not right for you.

You don't immediately need to quit your current commitments and put your financial obligations at risk. What this does mean, though, is that you need to stay curious, stay hungry for positive change, and keep taking steps towards the things that stimulate your mind, body and soul.

Don't worry about which step to take next, or how things will unfold for you. Remember, if you show your excitement to the Universe, it will give you more things to feel excited about. Wondrous opportunities will follow and help you to discover your path in life, as long as you act on the signs.

Small steps are fine, because they'll lead to bigger things. Eventually you'll work out a way to make your passion your paycheque. This could be an extension of what you're already doing or, if you're in a profession you dislike, it means you'll eventually be able to give it up and commit to your purpose full-time.

You were created with intention. You are here to help, love, assist, save and entertain. You are here to inspire and put a smile on someone's face. You are here to make a difference. You wouldn't be on this planet, at this time, if you didn't have something to offer.

There is a purpose behind your existence, and when you discover what it is, you will not only change the dynamics of the world, but also experience abundance in all areas of your life.

Money and greed

Money is merely energy – neither good nor bad, and unlimited in our infinitely abundant Universe. Make money to assist you, not to complete you.

Sometimes, people feel that it's wrong to make money by living their purpose, so let's take a moment to define what money really is. Before you say it's a token used to complete a transaction for goods or services, or anything along those lines, let me stop you. Money is simply energy!

Therefore, money is neither good nor bad. The label you give it is up to you, and the way we interpret money depends on how we attract positive situations or negative situations regarding money.

There are people who do great things with their money, while the way others use it can reflect the misery inside their minds. Money is simply an amplifier. If you're not trying to create value by spreading kindness and love when you have very little money, what makes you think you're going to do that when you have more of it?

Money flows to those who believe they deserve it and can attain it. Let me ask you right now, what are your views on money? Do you believe you deserve to have more money? Your subconscious thoughts and feelings on money will reveal a lot about your current reality and the one you'll experience if these perceptions stay the same.

Some say that money is the root of all evil, yet they still pray for it. That's like going to a Burger King, making an order then walking out before you've even been handed your meal. How can the Universe deliver a request you've already cancelled?

Some of us feel bad for wanting more money; we're told we're being greedy. Truthfully, most of us want money so that we can experience financial freedom and live our most desired lifestyles without restriction. This might include wanting to go on holiday with your loved ones whenever you want, and not having to worry about how much you spend while you're away. If you perceive this as greed because others will never get to live that lifestyle, you're assuming that a) the supply of money is limited and b) others will never break away from their current lifestyles to experience the same level of freedom.

Greed works on the basis that there's a limited supply of a particular thing and that you want the majority, which will consequently be at the expense of another person's wellbeing.

We are led to believe that there is only ever a limited supply of what we want, yet the truth is that abundance is infinitely available and provided by the Universe.

Limitation, then, is only a product of your mind. When your mentality is focused on what you lack, you project a fear-based vibration out into the Universe, which brings you more things to be scared about. You become scared to lose money, so you guard it closely. You become afraid to spend it, because you don't know if you'll have that much money again. As a result, even though you're trying your best to hold on to your money, your vibration may create an avenue to financial difficulties.

When we commit our energy to poverty, we manifest poverty. I'm not saying you shouldn't save your money, or that you should just throw it away. However, you should focus your mind on prosperity – there's power in believing and allowing wealth to flow to you.

Too often we're sold ideas around lack and limitation, when the truth is that we have creative power and control over our circumstances. When individuals can inject fear into the masses, the overall vibration of the collective consciousness projects yet more fear, poverty and destruction. It's an effective way to control humankind.

Money is readily available to everyone, and the distance between you and money is determined only by your attitude towards it. Remember, though, that money will only assist you, not complete you. It's not what gives you your life purpose. You can't add value to the world and serve others by accumulating lots of money. You must also have the desire to make a difference.

Achieving true happiness

Happiness doesn't come from other people, from places or things. It comes from within.

I've deliberately minimized the use of the word 'happiness' throughout the book so that I could leave it right until the end. I hope you can see that by raising your vibration and having feelings of joy, you're actually experiencing happiness.

We're led to believe that happiness is based on external influences: people, places or things. We have all these goals and desires in life, believing that once we achieve them, we'll be happy forever: when we find someone to love, we'll be happy; when we get our own house, we'll be happy; when we lose 20 pounds, we'll be happy. These may give you temporary happiness but this is fleeting – it doesn't stay with you. So once you acquire these things, you carry on pursuing lasting happiness from other external things.

Money, for example, is frequently linked to happiness and even success. But you'll learn from the richest people in the world that even with lots of money you can still experience sadness. If money was used to measure happiness and success, at what point would the scale begin and end? After all, numbers never end. You can easily want more and more, even once you identify your target. So you can't use it as a tool for measurement.

I explained at the beginning of this book that we pursue things because we believe they'll make us happy when we get them. The same applies to the money we want: we don't want the money itself, but we do want the security and freedom it will give us, because we believe that this will make us happy.

But if you were the only person on the planet and you had unlimited access to money, how useful would this be? How about being able to afford any holiday or crazy adventure you wanted, but having extremely poor health? What about being able to buy all that you ever wanted, but being neglected by the entire world? Or even being given an unlimited supply of money while working in the worst job ever, 20 hours a day?

Even your ideal partner has no control over your lasting happiness. They can only affect your relative happiness, which can vanish in seconds if external conditions change – if your partner acts in a way that you perceive as hurtful, for example.

The advertising industry is skilled at toying with your happiness because it preys on the knowledge that all of us want to be happy. 'Buy this and you'll be happy,' it says. You buy it, and then six months down the line they release a new version. You then realize that the previous product failed to give you long-lasting happiness, so you buy the new one in the hope that it will instead. The cycle repeats.

What if you could feel happy all the time? Isn't this the ultimate goal? It would mean that you're happy with what you've got *at any moment* – for the rest of your life. We could then say that lasting happiness is what true success looks like.

This is what true happiness is. It's lasting and it occurs when you remain at the highest frequency, despite everything that's happening at the surface level of your life. I believe that this is the place we all want to be at; where people and events are unable to change our emotional state from our natural state of love and joy.

To sustain happiness, you must work towards self-mastery. It's an inward journey that requires substantial spiritual growth. Choosing empowering thoughts over limiting ones should become your natural way of thinking. You must make it a habit to look on the bright side of things and let go of the past; to stop living in the future and appreciate where you are and what you have right now; to withdraw from comparisons, and love everything in this world without condition. Embrace what *is*. Be happy.

Final words

Going after a greater life is far from easy, and that's why most people settle for less. But if you take the time to absorb what you've learned in this book and start acting with determination, positivity and tenacity, you won't be one of those people. One small step at a time, you'll build unstoppable momentum and move ever closer to the life you've dreamed of living.

Remember that there's a lesson in every challenge, a lesson in every failure, which means your failures don't have to be failures at all; they're just twists in your path to greatness. If you commit your whole heart to achieving something and it doesn't work out, you can take that as a promise from the Universe that it wasn't the right thing for you. Something better is coming. Keep going.

Remember, too, to trust your instincts. Listen to that feeling in your belly that warns you about a toxic relationship. Listen to that voice in your head that lets you know when you're wasting your time. Respect your personal boundaries, and ask others to respect them, too. If something doesn't feel right, it very well might not be. And if something feels wonderfully, deeply, powerfully right, it probably is. Go with that. Let it flow.

Have faith. Let go of fear and your life will shift from ordinary to extraordinary. You'll connect with your higher purpose – because it's impossible not to when you're striving with every cell of your being to travel through life with a commitment to your personal growth.

You have everything you need to create an exciting and beautiful life, and it all begins with loving yourself. By building and maintaining a high vibration, you'll achieve your dreams. And even if it takes a long time, your high vibration will make you feel good along the way. That's all we really want, isn't it? To live a life that *feels good*.

I promise you that through dedication to loving yourself, you'll achieve the incredible. It might not be a stroll in the park. It may take time. You might have to make sacrifices to get further on your journey. But it will be worth it.

Over to you.

Vex King.

The author's mission

You might find this a bit strange, but on a number of occasions in my life, strangers have approached me to deliver messages similar to the one I'm bringing you in this book. When I was 21, I was approached in a bookshop. A middle-aged woman came up to me and said, 'You are blessed. You are close to God. You need to share your message with the world. You are going to help a lot of people.'

Another time, I was waiting for the train home after work. As I walked towards the end of the platform, all the people who were already standing there started to move away. This never normally happened (I actually sniffed myself to ensure there wasn't an unpleasant odour coming from me! I smelled fine.) Moments after, an old woman with a scarf on her head approached me out of the blue and asked me what I did for a living. As I answered the question, she interrupted me with the words, 'You're special.' Confused and concerned, I attempted to step away from her, but then she said,

'You have a lot of blessings from your past life, but you should also know what you've done wrong.'

I was slightly intrigued by this comment, so I carried on listening to this woman. She began to tell me what and who I apparently was in my past life. She claimed I was part of a special team in the military. She said I was one of the most valued soldiers and my country had benefited hugely from my successes, even though I'd hurt many people, too. She explained the implications of my behaviours in my supposed previous life.

Although it sounded bizarre, the story was extremely creative and captivating. She told me what I needed to do in this life to complete my mission. One thing she made very clear was not to let anger get the better of me, because it would lead me to failure, and she encouraged me to communicate positively to others because I could heal them.

At the time, I remember trying not to laugh because I found this all so weird. I was unconvinced and she caught a glimpse of this. Finally, she said, 'Well, you don't have to believe me, but any good advice is gold.' As those words came out of her mouth, the train approached the platform after an unexpected delay. I told her I had to go and walked towards the doors. She said goodbye – and then she said my name, even though I hadn't shared it with her. Once I'd got on the train I looked out of the window, but there was no sign of her.

Every time things like this occurred, I put it down to nothing more than strange coincidence. However, there have been countless occasions where things like this have happened that I haven't thought much of at the time – but things have now started to make sense. My pain has helped me to discover my passion, which has led me to identify my purpose. Deep down, what brings me the most joy is when I help people improve their lives. I love seeing people win.

Towards the end of 2015, I started an Instagram page to share my personal quotes and thoughts on life, love and purpose. My aim was spread positivity online. I recognized that this platform was free for the public and I could add value to a large number of people's lives without having to charge them money.

Within a few months I gained an increasing following as more and more people were drawn to my words. As my popularity grew, I was approached for advice by hundreds of people on a monthly basis because they admired my outlook on life. Here was an opportunity to coach people and guide them towards positive change.

Today I call myself a mind coach – someone who helps people to exercise a new way of thinking and to bring about a new and positive way of living. If you're interested in getting in touch, please visit my website at vexking.com.

Post pictures or your favourite images, pages,
quotes and experiences related to this book
on social media using **#VexKingBook** so I can
like them and feature them on my page.

Acknowledgements

Kaushal, my wife, my soulmate, my best friend, thank you not only for encouraging me to write this book, but also for inspiring me to share my words with the world. You have always believed in me and seen me for everything that I am, not for that which I'm not. My journey thus far would not have been possible without you. I could not ask for a better life partner.

Thank you to my dear sisters for all your help in raising me while having to put up with my mischievous ways. I know it was never easy, but I appreciate your patience while I was growing up. You've been there for me since the very beginning, experiencing some of our worst times together. Without you, I don't think I'd have been able to hang on and become the man am I today, passing on my wisdom to others.

To Jane, my agent, and the team at Hay House Publishers: thank you for believing in this book and in my vision to change the world through my words. Your hard work and support means everything to me. You've given me an opportunity to change the world for the better.

Finally, I'm genuinely grateful for my amazing followers on social media who support me and inspire me to keep sharing my perspectives. It's because of you, and for you, that I write this book.

Read on for an exclusive extract from *Healing Is the New High*, the #1 *Sunday Times* bestselling follow-up title from Vex King, which is now available from Hay House in tradepaper, e-book and audiobook formats.

We'd had an argument. I can't remember what it was about, but it was a big one. I had a funny feeling that night – unsettled, as if something big was going to happen. It could have been due to the argument, or discomfort rooted in paranoia – I knew she was heading out to a bar, and she always got plenty of attention.

On top of that, she hadn't texted me. I'd always get a text goodnight, even if we'd fallen out, but that night I got nothing. My mind was crowded – too many conflicting thoughts were blaring out – and I just couldn't sleep:

Maybe I've taken things too far.

Maybe something's happened to her.

I think I need to text her. No, wait – she was wrong, not me.

What if she's moved on already and she's with someone else?

No, she won't be – that's deceitful, and I know her. I can trust her because she loves me with all her heart. After all, she's the one who pursued me when I wasn't interested.

Finally, I plucked up the courage to text her goodnight.

She sent her response in the early hours of the morning. She poured her heart out to me, saying she loved me and wanted to patch things up. Apparently, her life wouldn't be the same without me.

I bought the idea, I really did.

But then a friend sent me a text, and in an instant, even before I'd opened it, I felt anxious. I just had a *bad* feeling. And I was right. The text said that my girlfriend had gone home with his cousin.

I felt angry and disappointed, but also doubtful. This particular friend didn't like the idea of the two of us and he had his reasons. Maybe he was trying to put me off her. But then, why would he lie? After all, the guy he was accusing of being with my girlfriend was his cousin. Also, my friend had existed in my world long before my girlfriend had, so I should have been able to trust him before I trusted her.

And to be honest, I owed it to him to believe him because I'd broken the 'Bro Code' by getting together with my girlfriend despite knowing he'd had history with her. Our love story was flawed to begin with and it should never have existed.

Eventually, I confronted her. And she was appalled. She denied it and told me my friend was jealous and trying to get between us. She made me feel bad for believing him and not trusting her. She seemed open and vulnerable, and told me she was deeply hurt. I felt guilty – she was that convincing.

And here was my problem. Every time we argued, a new story would emerge and the narrative would be the same. She was unfaithful to me on multiple occasions, and each time, she'd buy her way back into my life and emotionally manipulate me into believing her faults were my flaws.

This pattern was becoming embarrassing for me. I had a reputation as the boy who got the girl – not, perhaps, because I was good-looking but because I had a charming nature, was popular with my friends, and had a good heart. Now, I was becoming known as the boy with the girlfriend every other boy was hooking up with.

My closest friends had warned me; even strangers had. They told me to use her for what she was good for: physical intimacy. But I was in way too deep, and I didn't believe in being in a relationship if there was no future in it. I didn't want to hurt her. And I saw light within her that no one else could see.

People labeled me 'whipped' and 'sprung,' and eventually I responded to that by pretending to use my girlfriend for sexual encounters. But this was a lie. I felt as if I needed her. It was painful with her, but my life would seem more painful without her. The pain wasn't just emotional, either: I was getting into fights with other men over her. Men who teased me about what they were doing with her, and how I wasn't good enough for her because her attention was swaying toward them.

I'd always heard that it's guys who are the players, the scumbags, the ones who have all the control. But I'd lost mine. Here I was, a hopeless romantic foolishly believing in an illusion I'd shaped from my own imagination about this other person, and the connection I thought I could have with her.

As time went on and new evidence came to light, I finally hit boiling point. I knew I couldn't be with her, and that I had to remove myself from this relationship and not buy into her words and emotional manipulation.

I decided to put on a front. I told her that if we were to move forward with our relationship, she'd have to admit to everything she'd done. Deep down, I knew that nothing she could say would be enough because I'd already decided to move on, regardless of how uncomfortable it would be. But she didn't know this.

And her response really did put this into perspective. I wasn't even shocked as she told me about all the times she'd betrayed me – I'd always known it was true, but I'd just refused to accept it. I almost needed the words to come out of her mouth. What was increasingly painful at that point was the blame she put on me. In no way was I perfect, but she made me out to be a failure and created doubt in me, even though I'd been faithful and loving throughout our relationship. The only times I'd really given her a reason to look elsewhere was when we'd argued over my accusations of her cheating.

Afterward, it was so hard not to text her at night, like I always had. We'd had several breakups before this final one, and I'd always reopened our communication to get closure. However, what I was really doing was keeping my routine with her alive. I was reentering my comfort zone by speaking to her, even if it was just to argue.

So I had to exercise huge willpower to stop myself from responding to her text messages, which said things like:

'If you truly cared about me, you'd reply.'

'If you loved me at all, you'd want to work this out.'

'I miss you and will do anything to be with you.'

Nevertheless, this really was the final straw. The heartache was too great this time, and I was willing to undergo the pain of change in order to break my attachment to her. I had to resist the urge. I had to start a new chapter.

Although I didn't know it at the time, in the months following the breakup I went through a traumatic grief reaction and experienced a number of intense thoughts, physical sensations, and emotions. With traumatic loss it's really hard for the mind to wrap itself around the concept that this thing's really happened and that it's true. Below, I've described my symptoms and their trajectory:

Denial I was still a little unsure if this really was the end. I questioned whether or not we should actually try to make things work. I mean, if this was love, we shouldn't just give up on it.

Hatred Hate is a strong word and I don't like using it, but this is how I'd describe what I felt toward her. She'd embarrassed me, played me for a fool, and got in the way of my most important friendships. But I wasn't just angry with *her* – I felt anger toward a whole gender: women. I felt they couldn't be trusted, and that nice guys do indeed finish last.

Disappointment I went into a deep mode of overthinking – questioning why things hadn't worked out in the way I thought they should have. *What had gone wrong? Why had she done it? She'd said she loved me!*

And when she stopped sending me text messages – to which she was getting no response – I even said to myself: *If she really loved me, why would she let this end?*

Self-blame I went through a period where I blamed myself for the breakup. *Maybe if I'd paid more attention to her, she wouldn't have shifted her attention elsewhere*, I thought. I'd recall statements that she'd made, in order to evoke guilt in myself. I even began questioning my looks and my physical attributes, which just left me feeling even more insecure.

Anti-love I told myself I'd never love again and that I'd never commit to anyone. I actually convinced myself that I needed to become more of a player. Although this role wasn't in my nature, and I never quite fulfilled it, I did start to have more random hook-ups. But I often felt ashamed and disappointed in myself after them.

Moving through the pain toward healing

After the end of that relationship, I kept telling myself not to get too deep with people. I had a guard up, and as soon as I sensed I was falling for a girl or I felt threatened by one (as if she were going to hurt me), I tried to hurt her first and broke things off without giving her a chance. I had trust issues and I never admitted to them. If a girl had a close male friend, I'd assume the worst, and this created problems in my romantic relationships.

This often meant I wouldn't give girls the treatment they deserved, or that I was capable of. And although I believe that everything happens for a reason and things have worked out as they were meant to, I'm truly sorry that I inflicted my own pain and insecurities onto my romantic partners. I was always the one to end these relationships, but I take responsibility for the times when I didn't act with love, compassion, and understanding.

The truth is, after that breakup, I needed to undergo a whole healing process. The relationship had severely dented my belief in others and, more importantly, in myself. The flaws in my perception meant I could never love with all of my being. I was unable to turn up in a relationship with genuine love to give – I was always trying to receive love, and the moment I felt it wasn't being delivered in the way I wanted it to be, I'd switch off.

What I didn't know was that I was already healing. From the moment I made the difficult decision to end that relationship for good, every minute, every painful emotion, and every flicker of rage or doubt became vital to my ability to become the person I am today. The person I so badly wanted to be.

I'm not saying that I'm 'done' – there's always work to do and there'll always be wounds to acknowledge and heal. But when I started to take an active role in my own healing, I realized I'd started the work years earlier. I just hadn't known how to understand it, or how to interpret the moments of clarity I experienced, or how to *use* my emotions to propel me forward instead of becoming stuck in a hole.

Even in the early stages of my relationship with my wife, I acted on the pain of my past. Fortunately, my wife had the capacity – and the willingness – to hold space for me to heal in. It was my responsibility to commit to my healing journey, and also to hold space for hers, which she was equally devoted to. We were both grieving over past relationships. And although it took time, when I learnt to put my ego aside and welcome the potential of a new life, there was no going back.

Your journey toward healing

This isn't a book about relationships. Well, it is in a way, because relationships (not necessarily romantic ones) are always an important element of a person's healing journey. But I want to make it clear that I'm not sharing the story of this breakup with you because this book is about breakups. Instead, I'm sharing it to lay bare a little part of myself – to reveal a pain that I've felt, and healed from, in all its ugliness.

This story also reveals some of the things about myself that I've been most ashamed of over the years – paranoia, jealousy, ego, insecurity, and a willingness to believe lies because I didn't want to be alone. Being ready to reveal those darker parts of ourselves is vital if we want to draw light into our life again. And if I'm going to ask *you* to do it, you have to know that I'm willing to do it too.

My intention in this book is to give you the support and motivation necessary for you to embark on your personal journey to inner healing. I understand that some journeys will be harder than others. You might be healing from a relationship breakup, sure, but if you're healing from something else, you're welcome here too. If you've been through a traumatic experience that you still struggle to speak about, you're welcome here. And whether you're recommitting yourself to healing old emotional wounds or battling with something new and raw, you're welcome here.

You'll gain insight into your own lived experience, and discover opportunities to reflect on and see your pain in a new way. I won't pretend that every page will be easy to read, or that every moment of this journey will feel *good* to you – because the reality of inner healing is that it hurts. You have to face up to experiences and emotions that you've tried to squash, feelings that you've hidden away in the recesses of your mind.

You have to confront your own perspective on the world, on yourself, and on other people. And you must invite yourself to accept the possibility that you were wrong – that things weren't always the way you thought they were.

One thing I know about trauma is that it distorts and intensifies every negative thought, feeling, physical sensation and so on that we have. Trauma is like being covered with open wounds and wading into the ocean. A person who is whole and healed will very likely experience a positive sensation, especially if the water's warm and inviting and they love the ocean; however, someone who's experiencing trauma will immediately feel pain as the saltwater burns each wound. Trauma makes us thin-skinned, overly sensitive, hypervigilant, and prone to pain. And it's often all-encompassing, too, so our attention is focused on the pain and on desperately trying to avoid more of it.

When you experience the world through the lens of trauma, it's easy to miss the opportunity for positive experiences. Healing isn't a linear process – we move two steps forward and one step back on all levels. Gradually, healing can ripple out, like a stone tossed into a pool of still water; each ripple penetrates the trauma and replaces it with healing energy. Committing to the practices of healing is the first step. Be patient with yourself, get support where you can, and positive changes will occur without you even noticing.

No matter how skeptical or unsure you feel right now, you're here – reading these words and taking the first steps on your journey to powerful inner healing. You're doing it already, and with this book in your hands, you don't have to do it alone. Every chapter includes the gift of one or two practical exercises that will gradually lead you to a new sense of confidence and freedom. Each exercise is simple, and you'll learn how to integrate it into your daily life in a way that makes your healing process a part of your everyday.

Inner healing isn't something you do in the evenings or on weekends – you'll learn to work on it all the time. And I'll share more of myself along the way, of course; I'll tell you about the experiences that have helped me and that I hope will remind you that you're in good company.

One thing I know about trauma is that it distorts and intensifies every negative thought, feeling, and physical sensation we have. Trauma makes us thin-skinned, overly sensitive, hypervigilant, and prone to pain. And it's often all-encompassing, so our attention is focused on the pain and on desperately trying to avoid it.

If your attention is fading here, I'd like you to ask yourself why. Is there a voice inside your head saying, *This isn't for me – other people can heal, but I can't?* That voice is your pain talking – and it's wrong. Because here's the thing: inner healing isn't something that only 'healers' or 'spiritual people' can do. Every person is their own healer. *You're* your own healer – you have all of the tools for growth and change already within you, and this book will teach you how to use them.

You'll discover how to explore the edges of your experience with curiosity, not fear. And ask yourself questions that will begin to take down the walls you've built to protect yourself from being hurt, allowing you to walk with new ease through life.

Questions like...

- Why do I respond like that?
- Why is that particular memory so important to me?
- Why do I base my assumptions about the world on that memory, and not this other one?
- Who do I trust? Who *can* I trust?

- What would happen if I told someone this?
- How would I choose to live if I felt completely free?

So, come with me. I welcome you on this journey. And perhaps, soon, you'll be able to welcome *yourself* on the journey to true peace, every single day.

ABOUT THE AUTHOR

Vex King is a #1 *Sunday Times* best-selling author, a social media content creator and a mind coach. He experienced many challenges when he was growing up: his father died when Vex was just a baby, his family were often homeless and he grew up in troubled neighbourhoods where he regularly experienced violence and racism. Despite this, Vex successfully turned his whole life around and is now leading a revolution for the next generation of spiritual seekers.

As a major voice in the world of personal development, Vex shares deep spiritual knowledge in a way that's easy to understand, with stories from his own life, great inspirational quotes and practical solutions.

For more inspiration from Vex, follow his popular social media platforms (all @vexking) and sign up to his mailing list at vexking.com.

vexking.com

ISBN: 978-93-88302-69-2
Paperback

ISBN: 978-93-94613-38-6
Limited Edition Hardcover

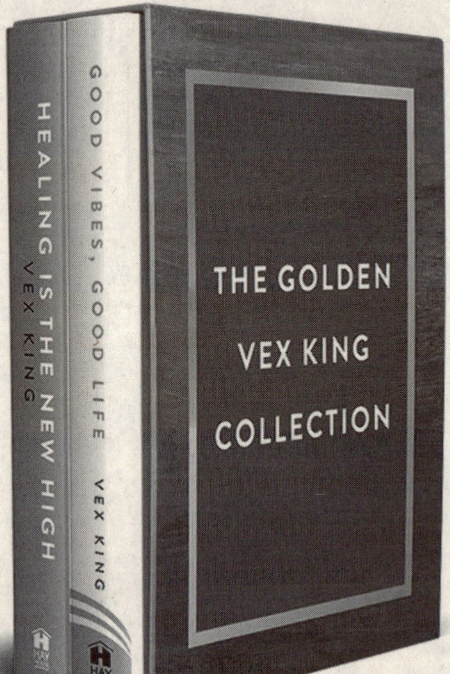

ISBN: 978-93-91067-55-7
Paperback Boxset

ISBN: 978-93-94613-39-3
Hardcover Boxset

'The gateways to wisdom and knowledge are always open.'

Louise Hay